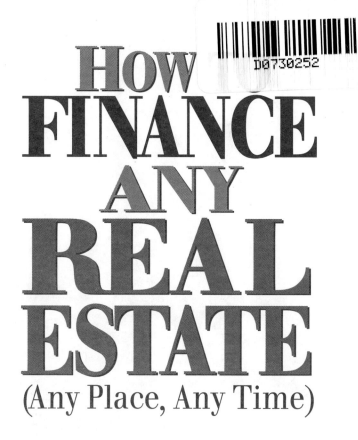

HOW FINANCE ANY REAL ESTATE

(Any Place, Any Time)

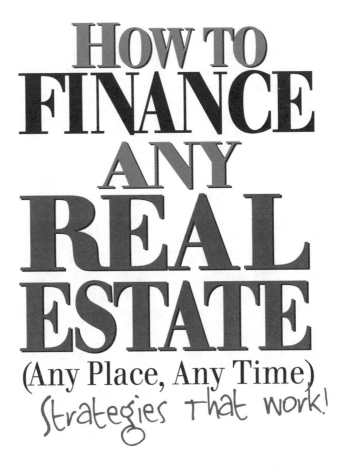

HOW TO FINANCE ANY REAL ESTATE

(Any Place, Any Time)
Strategies that work!

James A. Misko

SQUAREONE
FINANCE GUIDES

The strategies presented in this book are based upon the research and experiences of the author in his many years as a real estate professional. As you make your own investments, the author and publisher strongly suggest consulting appropriate professionals in the fields of law, real estate, and finance.

Because no investment strategy is foolproof, the authors and publishers are not responsible for any adverse consequences resulting from the use of any of the strategies discussed in the book. However, the publisher believes that this information should be made available to the public.

COVER DESIGNER: Phaedra Mastrocola
IN-HOUSE EDITOR: Joanne Abrams
TYPESETTER: Gary A. Rosenberg
COVER PHOTOS: Getty Images, Inc.
INTERIOR PHOTOS: Jack Bauer, jbauer@apartments24-7.com. "The premier interactive marketing system for apartment management."

Square One Publishers
115 Herricks Road
Garden City Park, NY 11040
(516) 535-2010 • (877) 900-BOOK
www.squareonepublishers.com

Library of Congress Cataloging-in-Publication Data
Misko, James A.
. How to finance any real estate, any place, any time : strategies that work / James A. Misko.
    p. cm. — (SquareOne finance guides)
    Includes index.
    ISBN 0-7570-0135-1 (pbk.)
1. Real estate business—Finance. I. Title. II. Series.
HD1379 .M62   2004
332.7'2—dc22   2003025038

Copyright © 2004 by James A. Misko

Printed in the United States of America

10   9   8   7   6   5   4   3   2

Contents

To the fun times with Bill Hickman, Jim Devereaux,
George Wingard, Don Furtick, and Wendell Hiatt,
who made me think outside the box.
And to Dick Reno, Hunter Quistgard, Kenny Johnson,
Cliff Weaver, Marvin Starr, and Ray Considine,
who showed me a whole world beyond the box.

Acknowledgments

No endeavor of this type can be completed without guidance and help, and this is where the grateful author expresses his appreciation to all who lent a hand.

Pat Rice, author of *IRA Wealth*, guided me to Square One Publishers and provided an abundance of invaluable information about IRA investments and more.

Phil Corso, past president of the Society of Exchange Counselors (SEC), shared his knowledge of current real estate websites and invited me to speak at the fortieth reunion of the Society. SEC is a great national organization that keeps real estate creative and interesting.

Rudy Shur agreed to publish this book, and then proceeded to change its point of view—and to make it a better book by far.

Joanne Abrams is an exacting editor who taught as much about editing as she learned about financing.

Patti Misko always had a smile on her face when she passed me working on the manuscript, and was as happy as I was when it was finished.

A Word About Terms & Monetary Examples

It's important to understand that some terms used in the field of real estate vary from region to region. Chief among these is the security instrument known as a *mortgage* in states east of the Mississippi; as a *deed of trust* or *trust deed* west of the Mississippi; and as a *land contract* in some parts of the Midwest. To make the text as easy to read as possible, the publisher has chosen to refer to this security instrument as a *mortgage* throughout the book. It's important to note, though, that any of these three instruments can be used along with any of the financing strategies presented within these pages. If you have any further questions regarding these or other terms that may vary regionally, please refer to the Glossary, which begins on page 167.

When making real estate investments, any of the individuals with whom you deal—from a real estate broker to a builder to a homeowner—is just as likely to be female as male. However, to avoid long and awkward phrasing within sentences, the publisher has chosen to use male pronouns throughout the book when referring to most of the participants in real estate transactions. This decision was in no way meant to diminish the skills and contributions of the many fine female professionals now working in the field of real estate, nor was it meant to ignore the many women now involved in successful real estate investments.

Finally, a word should be said about the monetary examples—house prices, for instance—that appear in the scenarios scattered throughout this book. Depending on where you live, these examples may seem unrealistically high or low. It's important to remember that real estate prices vary widely from state to state, and even from region to region within a single state. Please don't be put off by the monetary examples used. Remember that your focus should be on the financing strategies, and not on the prices. No matter where you live, you will find that the techniques offered in this book can be effectively used to finance your real estate ventures.

How to Finance Any Real Estate

(Any Place, Any Time)

Introduction

The strategies I am about to explain will guide you in buying, selling, and exchanging real estate in ways that have probably never occurred to you, and that are known to very few people. The fact is that you truly can finance virtually any real estate, any place, any time. This book will show you how it's done.

For over three decades, I have been a highly successful real estate professional. I have helped my clients finance investments in ways they never dreamed were possible, and have watched them build their real estate portfolios and enjoy their gains. And I have built up my own portfolio along the way. At first, I relied on conventional financing techniques, turning to banks and credit unions for the loans needed to complete transactions. But, as I soon learned, conventional financing isn't always available. Sometimes conventional lenders don't like the property being acquired. Sometimes they don't trust the borrower. And sometimes, while they're willing to provide the financing, they simply can't provide the *level* of financing needed by the buyer if he is to both purchase the property and make the necessary improvements. Fortunately, along the way, I also learned that there are a wealth of financing methods that can be used when regular financing channels are not available or not adequate. And each of these methods allows both parties—buyer and seller—to come out a winner. In fact, I discovered that this is one of the keys to successfully financing real estate deals. Every party in every transaction is looking for certain benefits. You know what you want—perhaps a home, an income-producing property, or a tax shelter. But what does the seller want? Immediate cash? A steady monthly income? A piece of property that better meets his investment needs? Figure out the benefits that each party is looking for, and you'll be able to choose a strategy that allows you to get the property you want.

How to Finance Any Real Estate, Any Place, Any Time presents forty-seven strategies, each of which either circumvents standard financing channels, or enables you to convince hesitant traditional lenders to supply the financing you require. Need time to acquire financing for a prime piece of income-producing real estate? Try securing the property with an option while you arrange for the loan. Have cash for only a small down payment, while the seller wants the security of a large down payment? Use collateral security—personal property such as automobiles, boats, or stocks and bonds—to provide the seller with the level of comfort he needs. Don't have cash available to cover the closing costs? Use notes or other real estate-backed paper instead. Can't afford that great property you need to house your new business? Buy only the building, and lease the land on which it's sited. Other topics include using a blanket mortgage or wraparound mortgage to obtain financing, forming a syndication, using zero coupon bonds and certificates of deposit to secure a loan, and much much more. All strategies are tried and true, and can be used to finance a variety of investments, from a personal residence to a modest apartment house to a sprawling retail shopping center.

While it's usually a lack of financing that stands between you and the property you want, I've learned that sometimes other problems exist. In cases in which the owner finances the purchase, sellers sometimes fear that if the buyer's income were to stop because of death, illness, or accident, the monthly mortgage payments might stop as well. In situations in which property is traded, some sellers are uncomfortable trading their property for real estate that has a second mortgage on it. That's why this book also includes a number of deal-making strategies—techniques that can be used when an obstacle other than financing stands between you and the property you want. You'll find that there are many proven ways to give the seller the benefits he's looking for, often without spending an extra dime on the investment.

Whether concerned with financing or deal-making, every strategy in this book is set up for maximum clarity. After a brief introduction, each first provides a "Strategy" section that presents clear step-by-step instructions for using that financing or deal-making technique. Following this, a scenario provides a true-life example, showing the strategy in action. Throughout, techniques are explained in easy-to-understand language, and definitions are provided as necessary. For further help, though, you can turn to the Glossary on page 167. Other helpful sections include a Resource List (page 181), which will guide you to groups and websites that can provide further information on real estate investments; a list of Selected IRA Trustees and Custodians (page 187), which will come in handy if you decide to use funds from your Individual Retirement Account to purchase real estate; and The Internal Revenue Service Code on Property Exchanges (page 189), which presents the rules for trading properties without paying capital gains tax. And throughout the book, insets present helpful information on tax strategies, owner financing, options, notes, syndication, due diligence, and many other important topics.

Before you start scanning *How to Finance,* looking for the best strategies for your real estate investments, a word should be said about the need to work with a team of qualified professionals. You probably already know that even the simplest transaction, such as the purchase of a home with the assistance of a bank loan, necessitates the use of an attorney. As you get involved in more complicated transactions, such as the trading of one property for another or the use of options and syndications, the need for truly qualified professionals will only increase. So if you haven't already found an experienced real estate attorney, accountant, and escrow closer, by all means, start your search. Advise all candidates that you will be using some less-than-conventional means of financing your purchases—strategies that are most certainly legal, but do not always involve conventional lenders. If the candidate tells you that it simply can't be done, walk away and look for someone else. Don't worry. There are plenty of good people out there who are ready, willing, and able to think "outside the box" and help you acquire the real estate you want.

Everyone has long appreciated the security provided by wise real estate investments. And if anyone needed a reminder, the recent sharp decline in the stock market certainly provided it! Unlike a stock, a piece of land can never totally lose its value. It simply won't cease to exist like so many dot-com companies did a few years back. The problem is that when a great real estate investment presents itself, you don't always have the resources available to seize the moment and make that property part of your growing portfolio. But as I have learned over the last thirty years, usually resources *are* in fact available. You just have to understand how to identify and use them. With *How to Finance Any Real Estate, Any Place, Any Time,* you will know how to put the wraps on virtually any real estate purchase—even when financing seems impossible. See you in escrow.

Exchanging Equity in a Home for Equity in Income-Producing Property

This strategy is designed to help you buy a champagne home on a beer income at no increased out-of-pocket costs. It involves exchanging equity in an old residence for equity in an income-producing property that generates sufficient revenue both to make payments on a more expensive home and to repay any loan.

The Strategy

Let's say you already own a house, but you want a better, more expensive home. Unfortunately, you find that your income is not sufficient to cover the increased payments. Your credit is good, however, and you have 30- to 50-percent equity in your current property—meaning that you still have to pay off a mortgage on 70 to 50 percent of the property.

Go to your banker and borrow the down payment for the desired house. The monthly mortgage payment on your new home will be higher than your current mortgage payment, so figure out how much more money you will need per month to make the new payment. Then exchange the equity in your current house for the down payment on an apartment house that generates enough spendable income to cover the difference between your present monthly mortgage payments and your new house payments, *and* repay the bank loan.

You will now have the home that you want. Moreover, you will have a *depreciation allowance* on the apartment house—an amount that you can deduct from your yearly taxable income based on the perceived loss of value due to the property's increasing age and resulting wear and tear. This allowance will lower your ordinary income tax on the revenue received from the property.

A Scenario

A realtor friend of mine had a client who owned a home appraised at $100,000. He owed $50,000 on the first mortgage, payable at $450 per month. The client and his family wanted a larger home in a better area, and really liked a house that was selling for $200,000. But when they examined their budget, they found that they were unable to squeeze out enough to make the additional $600 monthly payment it would take to get the new residence. They visited the house several times and after a month, when no one else had bought it, they went to the realtor with open minds.

The client was willing to do anything legal and reasonable to get that house. The realtor determined that the man's credit was spotless, verified his income and job security, and discussed with the sellers the possibility of a contract sale. The realtor then returned to the client and laid out his plan, which was accepted.

The next day, the client met the realtor at the bank, where they negotiated a $25,000 loan. The broker presented the $25,000 check to the sellers as a deposit for the down payment on the house. The broker agreed to accept his fee from the monthly house payments that would be made to the seller, who would carry back the note on the mortgage loan.

Next, the realtor took the $50,000 equity in the $100,000 house that his clients wanted to vacate, and contacted a builder who had a twelve-unit apartment house. The realtor used the equity in the house as a down payment on the apartment building, which—after expenses and mortgage payments—would show a spendable income of $1,100 a month. Again, the broker would take his fee out of the monthly payments his clients would be making to the builder, who would carry back the note.

The spendable income of $1,100 a month, plus the savings in nontaxed income from the apartments due to the depreciation allowance and interest deductions, was enough to let the family live comfortably in their new $200,000 house. It should be noted, though, that to keep the spendable cash flowing, the client had to manage the apartment house himself, perform some of the maintenance, clean the laundry room, and mow the lawn. That's why this strategy requires a buyer who is confident in his ability to perform all the functions necessary to make the arrangement work.

Understanding Owner Financing

It goes by many names—*owner financing, seller financing, seller carry-back, vendor take-back mortgage,* and *mortgage back*—but no matter what you call it, this technique is important for anyone involved in real estate, from a first-time homebuyer to a savvy real estate investor. The concept is simple. The seller of the property agrees to finance part or all of a real estate transaction by lending money to the buyer. In essence, the property owner assumes the role of the banker, and carries back the loan in the form of a note. As in any other sale, a down payment (if any) is negotiated between the seller and the buyer, and the buyer sends regular payments to the seller, typically on a monthly basis. About 20 percent of the houses sold in the United States involve some form of owner financing.

Owner financing is most often used when the buyer has difficulty qualifying for a conventional loan, such as a bank loan; when conventional financing is too expensive; or when the existing first mortgage may be assumed by the buyer, but the difference between the existing debt and sales price exceeds the resources of the buyer. In commercial lending, the borrower typically locates lending programs with rigid preset provisions, and applies for the most desirable set of terms. But owner financing is truly flexible, allowing the property owner and buyer to negotiate the down payment, if any; the interest rate; interest and payment adjustments, if any; balloon payment dates, if any; any *acceleration clause*—a provision giving the seller the right to declare the entire loan balance immediately due; and other provisions that a buyer would find it difficult to negotiate with a conventional lender. As long as the buyer and seller agree, the down payment can be skipped, or low monthly payments can be made until some future time, when the buyer is able to increase payment size or pay the loan off in full. Owner financing even allows for the inclusion of unusual terms in the note. For example, a payment may be set for the twenty-first of the month because the purchaser will use a paycheck from the sixteenth to make the loan payment. Or, if the buyer is a farmer, payments can be arranged to coincide with yearly crop sales.

Owner financing saves costs for both the property owner and the property buyer. It benefits the buyer by eliminating nearly all origination fees, thus saving from 2 to 5 percent of the total loan price. How does the seller benefit? By spreading the owner's capital gains over time, rather than giving him the lump sum he would receive from a conventionally financed mortgage, owner financing can sometimes prevent the seller from being bumped into a higher tax bracket, or can create time to take some capital losses as a means of offsetting gains. This technique further benefits the seller by providing good interest earnings. Although completely flexible, owner financing rates are typically higher than conventional home loan rates, and 4 to 5 percent higher than the rates offered by money market accounts.

Finally, owner financing benefits both parties by moving much more quickly than conventional financing, which can take a month or more. The owner-financed transaction can close as soon as the seller and buyer can agree on its terms.

While all of these benefits are important, you will probably find owner financing most appealing because its flexibility makes so many great investments possible. Within this book, Strategies 1, 40, and 41—to name just a few—show just how versatile this investment tool can be. As you learn more about it, you'll discover that owner financing can truly help you finance almost any real estate, any place, any time.

Trading Property You Don't Want for Property You Do

Most people today do not have large amounts of cash on hand. Cash is most often used in day-to-day transactions, and is not saved for large ones. But just because you don't have the cash needed for a down payment doesn't mean that you can't buy the property you want. As long as you have the wherewithal to make any monthly payments, a very simple solution may be at hand.

Instead of paying cash, you can offer personal possessions, and can even trade one piece of real property for another in lieu of a cash down payment. In fact, there's a whole world of people who specialize in exchanging real estate instead of buying and selling. All you have to do is offer something of cash value that you don't want—but that the seller does—in exchange for something you do. In a way, it's like trading one set of benefits for another.

The Strategy

Let's say that you have found a piece of property you want, but you don't have the ready cash to swing the transaction. Simply offer something that you own other than money—something that you have no use for. At the very worst, the seller will say "no." But he might say "maybe," "yes," or "let's see if we can work something out."

Any real estate can be offered, no matter where it is. Any personal property can be used, as well, including cars; jewelry; real estate contracts, notes, deeds of trust, or stocks and bonds; or coupons—prepaid meals, lodging, guided hunting trips, airline tickets, etc. As long as you own it and the buyer wants it, the deal will go through.

A Scenario

Years ago, my wife and I kept some horses on a fifty-acre piece of property in the country. The horses had become a big part of our lives, but it had started to be a real hassle to drive out once a day to feed and ride them. The solution, we decided, was to find a piece of property that was closer to our home and better suited to our needs.

My wife searched the real estate columns and found an ideal place. When we saw it, we found that it had everything we were looking for. The problem was that the owner wanted a large cash down payment. We balked. We did not have enough money put aside for such a property. Nevertheless, we liked it very much and continued to think about it.

Finally, we decided that if we wanted the property as much as we thought we did, we should at least make a proposal that we could live with. We offered our house equity subject to a loan, and some existing notes and first mortgages on land sales; and we offered to take out a new first mortgage on the "horse place" to get the owner some cash.

Although we knew that we had given the deal our best shot, we felt that the owner would reject the offer. He did not. He said "maybe." Then, after he had examined what we were offering, he agreed. We had gotten what we wanted by proposing an exchange when he had asked for cash. Our efforts were well rewarded.

The truth of the matter is that exchanging works very well. The only time you really need cash for your real estate is when you're leaving the real estate field. If you simply wish to move your equity to other properties for different benefits, an exchange will often suit you better than a sale, and, if done properly, may allow you to postpone or avoid paying capital gains tax.

Turning Your Problem Properties Into Cash

Real estate investors often own several properties that are not helping them reach their goals. But the fact that these properties don't currently have value for them doesn't mean that they won't have value for someone else. How can the investor put these properties to work, and use them to obtain real estate that will increase the value of his portfolio? That's what this strategy is all about.

The Strategy

You have in your portfolio several properties that, in various ways, are not performing as anticipated. Let's say, for example, that you have several free-and-clear lots of dubious value, and a small apartment house with negative cash flow. You placed these properties on the market some time ago, but nobody seems to want them.

There are two good ways to put these equities to work for you. First, along with the properties, offer any prospective buyer some solid real estate-backed notes that will provide him with enough cash flow to offset the negative cash flow on the properties. Similarly, you can create a note against another one of your properties, and use that to sweeten the pot.

An alternative strategy is to trade your problem properties for someone else's problem properties—provided, of course, that you feel you can turn the new properties around and make them worthwhile acquisitions, and that the other investor is truly motivated to dispose of his real estate. Structure your offer to give the other party a larger note and mortgage than the equities justify, but ask him to give you cash back. Then use the cash to remedy the problem property you are acquiring.

A Scenario

A group of local investors had formed a partnership. Their plan was to gain equity for five years and then sell the properties, taking capital gains on the profits. So far, they had acquired a duplex, a four-plex, scattered lots, and some small notes. These small items, which had a combined equity of $100,000, were gaining little in value. Moreover, the two buildings had a negative cash flow.

The partnership became aware of a condominium project that was being built by a local developer. The condo venture was in the depths of a depression. The owner had been involved in lawsuits for a year on the project, and had been paying the lender 18-percent interest. He had made no sales in more than a year, and had no money to proceed with construction. There was really nothing wrong with the project except the ownership. The owner knew it, and was highly motivated to rid himself of the property, which had a remaining equity of $300,000.

The partnership proposed to take over the condominium project. In exchange for his property, the developer would get the partnership's holdings, plus a note that was $150,000 greater than the difference between the two equities. He would then give some of the cash back at closing. The figures looked like this:

The partnership's scattered holdings:	$100,000
The condominium project :	$300,000
The difference in equity between the two sets of holdings:	$200,000
The note and mortgage given to the condo owner:	$350,000
The cash given to the partnership:	$100,000

The condo owner gave up the $100,000 cash for two reasons. First, he had received a note and mortgage for $150,000 more than his equity in return for the cash, so in a sense, he had bought the note at a discount. Second, he had rid himself of his problem property, which, after all, was his chief reason for making the trade.

Turning Your Dwindling Stocks Into Real Estate Equities

If you're like most investors, you've had the experience of purchasing stocks at a high price, and watching them fall in value. Now, the stocks are worth much less than their purchase price, and you want to be rid of them. But, understandably, you're reluctant to sell them for their present value.

Is there a way to trade those disappointing stocks for real property? Sure there is! Remember that those stocks still have a cash value—just not the value you hoped they would have. The trick is to find a property owner who is highly motivated to sell. Find him, and you'll be able to make a deal.

The Strategy

You have a portfolio of stocks, all of which have declined in value. You want to get out of the stock market and into the real estate market, but you hate the idea of taking a loss on all those stocks.

Look for a property owner who has holdings that you want and is highly motivated to sell—even if it means accepting less than the real estate's appraised price. If he's looking for cash but finding no cash market for his holdings, he's your man.

Now offer your stock to the owner of the real estate at its *original purchase price,* rather than its current value. If you have correctly determined the property owner's motivation, he will accept the offer, knowing that the stocks can be sold for quick cash.

A Scenario

Early in his investing days, an insurance broker had purchased bank stocks because they allowed him to get started with only small amounts of money. Naturally, he believed that the stocks would grow in value. But the stocks had risen from $20 or $30 a share to $40 and $45 a share, only to fall to $10 to $12 dollars a share when high interest rates forced banks to sacrifice much of their profits. He felt that real estate would be a much more secure investment, but needed to sell the stocks in order to get cash for his new venture. Unfortunately, his ego would not allow him to take that kind of loss.

Finally, I asked the investor if he would be interested in getting out of the stocks—for their purchase price—in exchange for real estate equities. He was very much interested.

Next, I found a developer badly in need of cash. He was trying to finish his work on a subdivision, had exhausted his first bank loan, and knew that getting a second loan was almost out of the question. I related my client's situation, explaining that the insurance broker wanted to invest in real estate and could supply stock that was readily salable—although it surely wouldn't sell for his asking price.

Since the developer had already made a healthy profit on several of the subdivision's developed lots, he agreed to accept the stocks at the old purchase price of $20 a share, even though he would receive, at best, only $12 a share on the current market. With that money, the developer was able to finish his project and enjoy a large profit on the remaining lots. Meanwhile, the investor received his original price for the stocks, and acquired equity in subdivision lots that he was able to sell at a nice profit some years later, after the property had appreciated in value.

Postdating a Sale to Secure One Property While Selling Another

O ne of the easiest techniques to understand and use is the postdated sale. When you want a piece of property but simply don't have sufficient cash on hand to make the purchase, this strategy will enable you to maintain control over the desired real estate while you secure the required money.

The Strategy

Let's say that you want to buy a piece of property, and are willing to sell a piece of real estate that you already own to finance the purchase. The seller refuses to exchange his property for yours. He wants cash.

Make a deposit, sometimes referred to as an *earnest money deposit,* and offer to purchase the property with a postdated completion date. Usually, unless you're paying an outstanding price, the seller will hold the property for ninety to a hundred and eighty days at the most.

Most *binders*—written agreements that accompany deposits— state that if the purchaser does not comply with the conditions of the binder, the deposit will be forfeited. So it's important to work twenty-four hours a day along with your realtor to sell the old property within the time limit. Use your friends, your relatives, and the realtor's clients. Tell everyone to talk about real estate wherever they go—specifically, about the property that is on the market. Once the property is sold, you will be able to complete the original transaction.

A Scenario

A client of mine wanted a particular farm very badly, being convinced that a major road would be built through the property in the future. The client was not affluent, and had tried every exchange offer he could muster—all with no success. At last, he plunked down a deposit of $2,000 with the provision that he would have ninety days to sell a piece of property he owned and pay the cash balance the seller required. The offer was accepted.

Between the farmer and my client, that property was advertised at every grange meeting, political meeting, council meeting, and any other meeting that would stand for the intrusion. It sold within the ninety-day period, and the purchase was completed.

Tax Strategies in Real Estate Financing

Through the course of a year, the average American earns *ordinary income* in the form of wages, interest, dividends, and/or net income from a business. All of this income is taxable. But against this income, certain exemptions and deductions are allowed, so that the average American ends up paying tax on a lesser amount than what he earned. Sounds good—except that many Americans are not fully aware of the tax benefits related to real estate investment, and do not take full advantage of them. The result is that they pay far more to the government than they should, and have far less cash available to profitably invest in real estate ventures.

This discussion looks at a number of tax deductions that are available to those who invest in real estate. It also highlights a strategy that can permit investors to build a solid real estate portfolio while avoiding the capital gains tax. Understand these tactics, using them as the government allows, and you'll be better able to finance any real estate, any place, any time.

Remember That Mortgage Interest Is Deductible

First, understand that in most cases, interest is tax-deductible as an expense. With the exception of interest paid on credit cards, which is not deductible, you can write off every dollar of interest paid, dollar for dollar against income. Let's say that you earn $100,000 in income in a single year, and during that same year, you pay $20,000 in interest. The $20,000 can be deducted from the $100,000, leaving only $80,000 in taxable income.

This makes it easy to understand why your biggest tax break is created by your monthly mortgage payments. For most people who acquire loans as a means of purchasing real estate, the bulk of each mortgage payment goes toward interest. And every bit of that interest is deductible.

And tax breaks go beyond your first mortgage. If you've used your real estate's growing value to pull out cash through refinancing or a home equity loan, that interest is also deductible.

Yes, leverage—the use of borrowed funds—has its problems. But as long as you create a backup for times of economic downturn, you should never be afraid of debt. In fact, the more you borrow, the greater your tax shelter will be.

Remember That Points Are Deductible

Points are the little added loan fees charged by lenders. The IRS defines points as any extra charges paid at closing in order to obtain a mortgage. Points are called by various names, including discount points, loan discounts, loan origination fees, and maximum loan charges.

Each point equals 1 percent of the loan principal. A $100,000 loan with two points, then, would cost the borrower $1,000 per point, for a total of $2,000. Because points are usually paid in return for a lower interest rate, they are really advance interest for the lender. Therefore, the IRS has stated that points are to be construed as interest, and are therefore fully deductible to the party who pays them.

Points paid on investment properties must be deducted over the life of the loan. But points paid on your primary residence are deductible in full the year in which the points are paid, as long as you meet the following requirements:

❑ The mortgage loan was used to purchase or build your primary residence.

❑ Points are an established practice in the region in which the loan was funded.

❑ The points paid were not in excess of the usual amount paid in that region.

❑ The points were not paid instead of normally separate costs, such as appraisal fees, title search or insurance, attorney's fees, or property taxes.

❑ The total points were not more than the total unborrowed funds, including the down payment and any escrow fees.

❏ The points were computed as a percentage of the loan principal.

❏ The points were listed as such on the mortgage settlement statement.

Even if you fail to meet all of the above restrictions, you can probably either spread the deduction out over the life of the loan, or reduce the total amount claimed as a deduction.

A final word should be said about points—and about interest as well. You can use far more than cash to pay points and interest. You can also use another person's note, a secured note, a mortgage, personal property, stocks, or bonds—really almost anything of value that the other party will accept.

Allocate Your Property's Basis Wisely

The original cost of any property, whether a home or an investment, is called its *cost basis.* With modifications for capital improvements, which raise the basis, and depreciation, which lowers the basis, this becomes your *adjusted basis.* At the eventual sale of your property, it is your adjusted basis that will be subtracted from the fair market value of your property—its sale price, in other words—resulting in the portion that will be taxed as capital gains.

Basis is divided by allocating a value to the land, personal property, and improvements such as buildings and parking lots. In most cases, you will come out ahead by allocating a low figure to the land, which is nondepreciable. This will leave more basis for personal property and buildings, which are depreciable, thus increasing the deductions for tax purposes.

Trade Property to Avoid Capital Gains Taxes

Whenever you sell one property in order to buy another, you pay capital gains tax on any profit received from your sale. How can you dispose of a property you don't want and acquire new property without paying taxes? Instead of selling the first property, simply exchange it for the second.

If you've read earlier strategies in this book, you know that I often advocate property exchanges as a means of acquiring real estate. This is a great way to get the property you want when you simply don't have sufficient cash on hand, and are unable or unwilling to borrow the funds needed. But exchanging properties has another advantage as well. According to Internal Revenue Code 1031, as long as you hold property for'the purpose of investment, and as long as you continue to pyramid upwards, always buying more expensive property and acquiring at least the same amount of debt, you can avoid paying capital gains tax. In reality, you are taking your capital gains with you to the next property without being taxed on it. That's why it's called a "tax deferred exchange." (To see this type of exchange in action, turn to Strategy 7 on page 27.)

A number of limitations have been placed on the sell-then-buy exchange, commonly known as the Starker exchange. In order for this transaction to be tax-free:

❑ You must identify your replacement property within 45 days of the sale of your old property, and must close the purchase of the new property within 180 days.

❑ Your replacement property must be *more expensive* than the property you've relinquished.

❑ You must take on at least as much debt as you've given up.

❑ Between the sale of the old property and the acquisition of the new, the proceeds of the sale must remain with an intermediary— a neutral agent such as an attorney, real estate broker, or escrow agent who's been engaged primarily to facilitate the exchange.

While the benefits of trading properties are many, it should be noted that the rules governing these transactions have been somewhat simplified here. (To read the full IRS code, turn to page 189.) To make sure that your exchanges are properly structured, you'll want to seek both legal and tax accounting advice. Qualified professionals can ensure that the transaction goes through without creating a taxable event.

Securing a Tax Shelter and Income Through Overtrading

S ometimes, large holdings in raw land can become a problem. First of all, the property provides little tax shelter. The
interest payments and taxes are deductible from other
investment income, but no depreciation allowance is available.
Second, despite excellent research performed before the purchase,
such holdings don't always perform as expected. The result is that
while you must keep making monthly payments on the land, the
land fails to produce any spendable income.

If the raw land you're holding is not providing you with the
benefits you now need, realize that you may be able to exchange
your large equity for a small equity plus cash, and thus find both the
tax shelter you want and the income you require. The challenge is
to find another investor with different problems and different needs.

The Strategy

Let's say that you have large holdings in raw land. While the land
may someday be in demand, right now, it is not moving, nor is it
providing you with a tax shelter. You would love some spendable
income, but all your money is tied up in your vacant property.

To solve your problem, look for an investor who has income
property that is less expensive and has a smaller equity than
yours, and who is sick and tired of tenants, maintenance, munic-

ipal inspectors, and the like. To balance the equities, he will use a note and second mortgage to pay you the difference between the two properties.

A Scenario

I was general partner of a syndicate that had a huge inventory of building lots. Unfortunately, though, the lots were not selling well.

At the same time, most of the apartment houses in town had 20- to 30-percent vacancies. The owners of these apartments were tired of the fluctuating amounts of monthly income they received from renters, and of never knowing how much they would have to spend each month to keep their buildings afloat. Both the syndicate and the apartment house owners were ready for a change.

The syndicate offered to exchange $300,000 equity in their lots for $150,000 equity in a twenty-four-unit apartment building. To balance the equities, the owner of the apartment house agreed to give the syndicate a $150,000 note and mortgage on the lots, payable on a quarterly basis.

After closing, both sides gave a great sigh of relief. The apartment house owner knew he that would not get any more telephone calls about maintenance, have to speak to the woman in apartment 12 about her noisy parties, or have to call a tow truck to remove a junk car left in the parking lot by a departing tenant. He could relax and listen to the peace and quiet of his lots. Tomorrow, he would plan a course of action to exchange the lots, one at a time, for property that would bring him greater benefits.

The syndicate members jumped for joy. They had rid themselves of a large number of unsold lots, and instead owned an apartment house, which they immediately turned over to professional management that would respond to the daily needs of the tenants. Of course, everyone's troubles were not over immediately. For a time, the syndicate had the problem of renting the vacant apartments, and the buyer of the lots had the problem of making his quarterly payments. Fortunately, both the apartment house market and the lot market eventually improved, and both parties reaped the benefits of the trade.

Selling and Reinvesting Without Tax Consequences

I f you're like many real estate investors, at various times, you have sought to exchange one piece of property for another. But sometimes, although you want "out" of the property you now own, you are not yet able to close the deal on your new real estate acquisition. And other times, you may not be at all sure about what you want to do with the cash you're about to receive from your current property. Between the sale of the old property and the purchase of the new one, you are understandably reluctant to pay the capital gains taxes associated with selling or with exchanging improperly.

Fortunately, since the 1979 court case *Starker v. United States*, Section 1031 of the Internal Revenue Code has provided an excellent solution to this problem. According to what has become known as the *Starker exchange,* you can make a tax-free exchange of properties as long as you identify the property you are to receive within 45 days of giving up ownership of your original property, you close within 180 days, and the new property is greater in value and debt than the old property. Between the sale of the old property and the acquisition of the new, the proceeds from the sale must remain with a neutral intermediary. In effect, the property exchange is held in suspension until the final purchase is made. (For more information on the Starker exchange, see pages 23 to 24.)

The Strategy

You are the owner of a parcel of raw land, which has been very hard to move. Suddenly, you find an investor who wants to purchase the property at an excellent price. You know you want to make the sale, and you also know that, as quickly as possible, you want to use the proceeds of the sale to buy a replacement property—without paying taxes on your initial gains. However, you have not yet found a replacement property.

To use the Starker exchange, first hire a facilitator—a neutral agent such as an escrow agent, attorney, or real estate broker engaged primarily to facilitate the exchange. After you sell your property, the facilitator will accept the cash from the sale and hold it while you find a suitable replacement property within the 45-day time limit.

When you find the property you want, write an offer to purchase, naming the facilitator as the buyer of the property. The facilitator will be paid a flat fee, and in most cases, will keep the interest the money earns between the two transactions, although this is negotiable. At the closing, which must take place within 180 days of your sale of the first property, title of the new property will pass to you. You will not have to pay capital gains taxes on the sale of your initial property. In fact, as long as you keep exchanging properties in accordance with the Starker exchange, you will be able to defer paying capital gains tax until you sell your last investment property. It should be noted, though, that the rules governing this type of transaction are complex, and the Internal Revenue Service has made it clear that the legal requirements for a successful exchange must be followed to the letter. For that reason, it is vital to seek both legal and tax accounting advice before proceeding with a Starker transaction.

A Scenario

A client of mine had acquired a high-end apartment house in Hawaii that provided him with a cash flow of some $20,000 per month. Several years after his purchase of the property, he began receiving verbal and written offers which showed that his equity had increased to somewhere in the neighborhood of $2,500,000. The time was right to sell.

An Alaskan broker had five buildings owned by a client for sale at $7,500,000, all with short-term bank loans. These properties had been put together by a corporation as part of its investment program, and the corporation had decided to sell off these holdings and concentrate on other activities.

My client, working with a broker in Hawaii, produced a cash sale for his apartments, with the expressed intention of exchanging them tax-free for the five Alaska properties. The cash sale was closed on the apartments, with the facilitator holding the funds. Then a closing date was set in Alaska to purchase the five buildings.

A local bank provided a short-term bridge loan for $5,000,000, and together with the cash from the earlier sale, the purchase was closed 30 days after the Hawaii transaction. The new owner now nets approximately $44,000 a month with the same equity he had in the Hawaii apartments. Moreover, because of his successful use of the Starker exchange, he did not have to pay capital gains taxes on the profitable sale of his apartment house.

Capitalizing
on Interest

There are many, many ways to structure a real estate purchase, and what is a good fit for one buyer is not necessarily a good fit for another. This strategy demonstrates one way of structuring a purchase that can work when you feel that the property you are buying will eventually appreciate in value, but in the meantime, you're interested in a tax write-off. The seller will benefit from this strategy, too, because the unconventional payment schedule will increase the amount he ultimately receives for his property.

The Strategy

You have found a piece of unimproved land that you feel will ultimately increase in value due to the expansion of an adjacent industrial area. At the same time, you are paying high taxes on your various income properties, and wish for an investment that would provide you with substantial yearly tax deductions.

Approach the owner of the raw land, and offer a sizeable down payment, followed by *no payments for two years*. After the two-year break, you will make payments at a market or above-market interest rate. During the break, of course, interest debt will accrue, so that when payments begin, they will consist almost exclusively of interest—all of which will be tax-deductible.

Naturally, not every seller will be interested in this type of arrangement. However, you will find that builders, land subdividers, investment groups, and elderly sellers often appreciate a long-term payment schedule that includes interest and capital gains. And, of course, due to the two-year buildup of interest, the seller will eventually receive more money than he would have received from a more conventional arrangement.

A Scenario

A client was interested in a portion of a subdivision that was under development. The syndication that owned the subdivision needed immediate cash to complete the installation of utilities, and additional monthly payments to help carry the debt on the property. Thus, it had offered some of the more desirable land for sale. My client felt that the offered land would increase in value over time. He did not, however, have a great deal of cash on hand to make the purchase.

I knew that the syndication had thus far received no offers. Therefore, I didn't hesitate to propose a smallish down payment and equally small monthly payments. The syndication, however, countered with requests for more money in both departments.

Although the sellers wanted both a down payment and monthly checks thereafter, I knew that their greatest interest was in getting an immediate infusion of cash so that they could complete their project. Since my client's resources were limited at the time, I came up with a different kind of offer—a larger down payment followed by no payments for two years. After that, my client would make good-sized quarterly payments at an interest rate that was above what the syndication was paying on its own loan. At the end of the two years, my client would have built up so much interest debt that his quarterly payment would be 99 percent interest, and therefore mostly tax-deductible.

The syndication agreed to the offer, provided that the full debt would be satisfied by an eight-year balloon payment. We countered with ten years, and the deal was closed.

Supporting a Small Down Payment With Collateral Security

This strategy is useful when you want to purchase a piece of property, and you have good security and a good job, but you simply can't come up with the large down payment desired by the seller. In such a case, *collateral security*—additional security supplied in the form of personal property such as automobiles, boats, farm equipment, stocks and bonds, real estate mortgages or contracts, and the like—can often be used to make the seller feel that the transaction is a solid one.

The Strategy

Let's say that you want to purchase a piece of property, but the seller demands a large down payment, while you are able to make only a small one. On the other hand, you have personal property that is of value—perhaps a car, a boat, jewelry, furniture, or livestock. And you own it all free and clear.

Simply have your attorney or escrow closer draw up a *chattel mortgage,* which is sometimes referred to as an asset-based mortgage. This document will pledge some of your personal property as security for the debt owed. The agreement can be structured so that the property is released after a certain amount has been paid on the principal. The agreement can also be arranged to fit the particular property being used to secure the debt. If the property being used for security is immature livestock or crops, for instance—something that will be marketed at a future date—the payments can be due a reasonable time after the usual marketing period.

Note that the property is not given to the seller, but is pledged so that if you fail to make your payments, the seller will be able to take possession of the property and keep it in lieu of the payments, or sell it and use the money to cover damages. If, however, you make the payments as stipulated in the agreement, the pledged property will be released from the lien.

The type of property you use for collateral security is limited only by your imagination, your assets, and your willingness to use your possessions to gain the benefits of ownership. Not just items like cars and boats, but also paper—other contracts, mortgages, or stocks and bonds—can provide security for a small down payment. The income from contracts, mortgages, or personal note collections can often be pledged as additional security.

A Scenario

A young client wanted to buy a $300,000 commercial property, and offered a note and second mortgage of $100,000 for exchange on the property. The seller, however, felt that the possibilities of default on the $100,000 paper were too high. This, coupled with the fact that the seller wished to retire trouble-free, caused him to reject the exchange offer.

After consultation with my client, I presented an offer that included no down payment on the $300,000 property, but used the $100,000 note and second mortgage as collateral security that would be forfeited if my client defaulted on his contract with the seller. It was accepted.

The seller retired to his mobile home, and the payments were made out of my client's income from the $300,000 property. My client continued to enjoy the additional income of $1,000 a month from the $100,000 note and second mortgage, which, he knows, he will be able to draw upon in the event of vacancies or lower rents.

Using a Certificate of Deposit to Obtain a Loan

Sometimes, circumstances cause lenders to be leery of giving borrowers the loan they need for a real estate venture. Perhaps the borrower is a stranger from another area, or perhaps the property behind the loan is old and in disrepair, and the lender doesn't feel that it offers the security he needs. Whatever the reason for the hesitancy, the lender can often overcome this obstacle by opening a certificate of deposit (CD) at the lending institution.

A *certificate of deposit* is a type of savings account in which a specified sum of money is deposited for a set period of time in a bank, savings and loan association, or credit union, and yields a fixed return. CDs generally earn higher interest than passbook-type savings accounts because the bank or other institution knows how long the money will be available to them, and can therefore plan on lending that money for a longer period of time, and thus earn more money. Some of the additional earnings are passed on to the depositor.

Opening a CD with your lender will give him additional security for your loan, over and above the property that backs the loan, and will generally make him happy by increasing his deposits and making his bank grow. The result is that you'll get the loan you need.

The Strategy

Let's say that you own a rental house in a coastal resort area that is a hundred miles away from your residence. You want to put a second mortgage on the house in order to fund another investment, but the local bank refuses to give loans to non-occupant owners, as during the winter season, when most rental houses in the area are unoccupied, vandalism and disrepair through neglect and wet weather take their toll.

Offer to open a certificate of deposit at the bank under the condition that the bank will make you the loan you are seeking. The amount you choose to put into the CD is a matter of judgment and accommodation, but try to deposit the bare minimum—certainly no more than 5 to 10 percent of the requested loan amount. Start low, and see what it takes to make the lender smile. Generally, the lending agency will ask for the CD to be pledged as additional security for the loan. If so, negotiate for the release of the CD as collateral after the loan has been reduced to a certain point.

Another option is to promise the lender that you will use the proceeds from the loan to open a CD in the amount of $15,000 to $30,000, if it is not to be pledged for additional security for the loan. You can then ask another banker for a loan in the same amount as the CD, using the CD as security. This will provide you with the full amount of cash you need for your venture. Moreover, you will know exactly where you'll be able to get the cash to make that loan payment when it comes due.

Be aware that you can't abuse this strategy. Some people deposit the CD, get the loan, and then pull the CD out, leaving the banker without any security. Most lenders now make it very difficult to pull the CD out before the designated time unless the depositor can prove hardship and a real need for the cash.

A Scenario

A friend of mine owned an old house that had been converted into four rental units. Behind the house was a twenty-year-old eight-unit apartment building in a bad state of repair. His mortgage payments were at $1,600 a month, but because of the disrepair, his earnings had dropped below the point where he could afford his monthly payments. He knew that he must either renovate the apartment house so that the rent would pay the debt, or reduce the monthly payments to make them more affordable. He chose the former course.

To finance the renovations, my friend wanted an $80,000 loan payable at $800 to $850 a month. However, no lenders were willing to make a loan on his run-down property. My friend then approached a lender and offered to open a CD in the amount of $20,000 for one year in return for a loan commitment on the terms he was seeking. The bank loaned him the $80,000 at 11-percent interest, and he opened a CD that earned 10-percent interest. My friend was a happy man. Sure, he had to deposit money in the bank to get the loan. But he earned the market interest rate and got a loan that otherwise would have been denied.

Using Zero Coupon Bonds to Secure a Loan

A number of the strategies presented in this book describe ways to persuade hesitant investors to provide financing for a real estate venture. One great tactic is to borrow more money than you need for the investment, and use the excess cash to purchase *zero coupon bonds*—bonds that pay no interest during the life of the bond, but are sold at a substantial discount and, though the buildup of accrued interest, pay face value when they reach maturity. Available for a fraction of their ultimate redemption value, zero coupon bonds will guarantee the return of the investors' money in the event that the property does not perform as well as anticipated.

The Strategy

You have found an apartment house that promises excellent cash flow. The problem is that you don't have sufficient money for the down payment.

Contact individual investors and ask to borrow the money you need for the down payment, *plus* the money you need to buy zero coupon bonds with a face value equal to the down payment. As security, then, you will offer the lenders your personal note, the cash flow from the property, and zero coupon bonds in the same amount as the loan.

Once you get a commitment from the investors, contact your stockbroker and buy zero coupon bonds in the amount needed. You should be able to get them for 50 percent or less of their face value, and will want to find bonds that will reach maturity when the investors' loan is due.

In the worst possible scenario, the property won't perform well, and the lenders will get back their original capital when the bonds mature. More likely, the property's cash flow will allow you to return both their capital and their interest, and you will be able to keep the bonds when they reach maturity.

A Scenario

After Alaska's 1986 real estate crash, there was plenty of property for sale, not only by individuals, but also by banks; the Federal Deposit Insurance Corporation (FDIC); and the Resolution Trust Corporation (RTC), which had taken over the fourteen failed banks and savings and loan associations in Anchorage. Properties were selling for considerably less than *replacement cost*—the cost of constructing a replacement structure.

I found a building available for a $100,000 down payment, but all the investors I contacted were having trouble with their existing real estate loans, and were not interested in lending further money. I soon realized that to give them the security they needed, I would have to do something a little different.

I decided to buy $100,000 of zero coupon bonds for 56 percent of their face value—$56,000, in other words. The bonds would mature in ten years, when the final loan payments were due. I therefore needed $156,000—$100,000 for the down payment, and $56,000 for the bonds. My approach to the investors was this:

1. Invest some portion of the $156,000, and I will pledge to you all of the anticipated cash flow from the building as first payment of interest.

2. I will pledge you the equity in the building $100,000+ and my personal guarantee on the loans.

3. If all else fails, the zero coupon bonds will pay you back your original investment capital.

The money came in, and I closed the transaction. I was so intent on arranging the financing that I almost missed the fact that if the property had the promised cash flow, at the end of ten years, the investors would enjoy good returns, and I would become the holder of the bonds. That would reduce the interest rate on the overborrowing to only about 2 percent.

Deal-Making Strategy
Using Insurance to Support the Purchase of Property

Many people depend on their income for survival. If their income were to stop because of death, illness, or accident, and any real estate properties they owned did not produce sufficient income to cover expenses, their ability to pay their monthly mortgage payments would stop as well—and the property could be lost. This, of course, is of concern not just to those who are purchasing real estate, but also to sellers, who fear that buyers won't make good on their contracts. Fear of the inability to pay can stop a buyer from making a purchase, and stop a seller from completing a transaction.

Fortunately, life insurance companies offer a myriad of policies that can cure these situations, providing security for people on both sides of the contract of sale.

The Strategy

Let's say that you wish to buy a piece of property, but either you or the seller is worried that you will not be able to make mortgage payments in the event of illness, accident, or death. Several types of insurance are available, each of which is appropriate in certain circumstances.

If the seller is concerned that you will default in the case of accident or sickness, contact a life or casualty insurance agent and buy a *sickness and accident policy* that will provide enough money to cover payments on the property even if your income comes to a halt. These funds can be assigned to the seller in the event that payments are not made.

If the seller is worried that mortgage payments will stop in the event of your death, a good solution is to purchase *decreasing term life insurance.* Designed for people whose financial needs are expected to decrease over time, this insurance reduces the lump sum paid at death over the term of the plan, and therefore is an excellent means of covering the amount of the mortgage as it is paid off. Some insurance agents are even able to devise an ordinary life policy that builds up a cash value over the years, and allows you to borrow from this pool of cash to make the insurance premium payments. If you *don't* borrow the funds, you will have a usable policy after the mortgage on the property has been paid off. This is often available at the same cost as decreasing term insurance, and is far more valuable in the end.

Another means of covering payments in the event of death is *mortgage cancellation insurance.* Also called personal mortgage insurance, or PMI, this type of policy was designed to protect the mortgage holder against default in the event of the homeowner's death, and can cover 100 percent of the cost of the property. Mortgage cancellation insurance is quite cost-effective, as if you later decide to sell the property, your insurance premium can be pro-rated so that you are charged only for the time the coverage was used.

A Scenario

A long-time client of mine—a fifty-year-old doctor—enjoyed a good income, but had done very little to build his estate. His income taxes had become unbearable, and he needed my help. Fortunately, among my listings was a client who wanted to sell an apartment building to raise cash.

The property was listed for $500,000, and the doctor made an offer at that price. He wanted to put no money down, but to assume the first mortgage of $350,000, and pay the seller the balance of $150,000 at $2,000 per month.

When the seller was informed of the offer, he sputtered and stammered a bit because he was looking forward to some cash. But he also had a definite use for the $2,000 per month, which was more income than the apartments were providing at that time. The seller thought about it overnight, and then accepted the offer with the provision that the doctor purchase a sickness and accident policy that would pay the mortgage in the event he became ill or incapacitated, and a life insurance policy that would pay off the loan balance should the doctor die prematurely.

The doctor had no health problems and breezed through the physical examination. He obtained $350,000 worth of life insurance on a decreasing term basis, as well as a sickness and accident policy that would cover the mortgage payments in the event of his disability.

Because of the doctor's high income, the premiums were easy to pay. The insurance was well worth the price, too, because if the doctor died, the property would be paid down to the first mortgage, and would provide his family with $3,000 a month spendable income. The tax benefits that he had originally sought accrued to him through his ability to write off interest payments, and through the depreciation allowance that permitted him to deduct money from his yearly income based on the apartment house's increasing age.

Gaining Appreciation and Working Time by Using an Option

The *option* is a written, recordable right to purchase property under certain terms and conditions, within a specified period of time. When you buy an option, you get the exclusive right to purchase property at previously agreed-upon terms—including an agreed-upon price.

The option is a marvelous tool when you locate a property that you want to buy, but you need time to find financing, to arrange for zoning changes, or to solve any other problem that is keeping you from reaching your goal. The option is also helpful when you find a property that you think may prove a good investment, but you know that only time will show its true worth. By paying a relatively small amount of money, the option will permit you to gain control of the property. And because the option locks in the price, you will never have to pay more than the amount specified in the agreement—not even if the property doubles or triples in value! Meanwhile, you will pay no taxes, no interest, no principal, and no carrying charges for as long as the option remains in effect.

The Strategy

Let's say that you are made aware of a parcel of raw land that is up for sale. You have also heard that a highway is being extended, and that one of the exits will be adjacent to that piece of property.

If the highway construction goes through, that real estate will be *path of progress* land, meaning that it will be property toward which development and industry are moving. In that case, the land will be worth far more than the asking price. The only problem is that it is not yet certain if the road will be built. Moreover, at this point, the price is beyond your means.

First, consider the amount of time you will need to discover if the purchase makes sense, and structure the option agreement around that time. If you find that the decision on the highway will be made within three years, have your attorney draw up an option to purchase the land within three years. The option document must, of course, specify the *option consideration*—the cash or property you will give to the property owner to secure the option. You might, for instance, offer $2,000 a year as option consideration. But option considerations can also be set to vary from year to year. If you know that the value of the property will be increasing each year due to improvements being made on the land, for example, you may feel comfortable putting up larger amounts as time goes by. Moreover, it is often possible to make a one-time option payment rather than a series of regularly scheduled payments.

In some cases, you may not want the property owner to get wind of your reason for wanting the option. If, for instance, the owner hears about the plans for the highway, the deal may disappear. However, if the seller is highly motivated to dispose of his property, and you need time to obtain a variance from the department of building or to secure financing, it may be in your best interests to let the owner know what's gong on, as this may help persuade him to consider an option as a good alternative to an outright sale.

Option payments can be structured to reduce the principal so that if you ultimately decide to make the purchase, the sales price will have decreased over time. If at any point you don't see the advantage of continuing the option, you can simply fail to make future option payments. It won't affect your credit in any way.

Finally, realize that although option payments are most often made in cash, any personal property—including jewelry, cars, boats, motorcycles, artwork, other real estate, or notes—can be used as option consideration. You are limited only by your imagination, your assets, and the willingness of the buyer to accept your property in lieu of money.

A Scenario

Years ago, I was presented with an eight-acre site that seemed as if it had been designed for an apartment house. It was not zoned for multiresidential buildings, but it had everything else in the world going for it.

The sellers consisted of a widow and her son. The asking price was $780,000. For $1,000, I was able to buy a one-year option, after which it was to cost me $5,000 per quarter until the new zoning was approved.

The option held the property for me while I completed the various tests and studies required to get the zoning approved. Nearly three years later, when the transaction was completed, the property's value was close to $1,200,000. The project had received approval for 125 units, and the price had been reduced to $700,000 due to the county's taking some wetlands. In addition to the quarterly payments I had made in option consideration, which were deducted from the total price, I had spent $135,000 on tests, studies, and lawyer's fees. But even so, my final cost was only $835,000.

Understanding the Option

Both Strategies 13 and 14 explore the benefits of using options. By putting you in control of the sale of a property, an option can often be used to buy the time you need to surmount a host of obstacles, from insufficient financing to problematic zoning. An option can also give you a chance to watch the movement of area property values before making a purchase. It can even allow you to offer an inflated asking price—and then wait for the property's value to catch up to the price before making the actual purchase.

Because the option is such a valuable tool for the real estate investor, it pays to understand how it works. As explained on page 47, the option is a written right to purchase a property under certain terms and conditions, within a specified period of time. In return for the option, you pay an option consideration—cash or other property—either as a one-time payment or as a series of payments.

As long as you, the buyer, keep to the terms of the agreement, and as long as the option has not expired, you have the exclusive right to purchase the property at the agreed-upon terms, or to sell the option to somebody else. No one—not even the property owner—can legally sell that property without first satisfying your option. Moreover, as long as the option is in effect, it is usually the property owner, not you, who is responsible for paying all of the inherent costs of the property, including taxes, assessment, and maintenance. Of course, until you exercise your option, the owner also has the right to use his real estate as he sees fit, as long as it does not violate the terms of your agreement. But you have a great deal of influence on the sale of the property.

Clearly, your goal when buying an option is to choose property that already has the value that you want, or that promises to appreciate in value. You might, for instance, choose a piece of property that is in the *path of progress*—property located in an area toward which development is moving—and wait for the land to appreciate as the area around it is developed. But one of the beauties of the option is that if the property does not perform as expected—or, for that matter, if you are unable to acquire the funding you need—you can back out of the purchase without any consequence whatsoever, other than losing whatever option consideration you have paid to that point. Once you fail to make the payments or to exercise your option to buy, all of the rights will simply revert to the property owner.

Satisfying a Demanding
Seller by Using an Option

Often, sellers are not realistic about current market values. They want tomorrow's price—not today's—for their property. And they're not about to part with their real estate until they get the price they desire.

When you believe that a piece of property will be valuable down the road, but the asking price is more than the real estate is currently worth, the option—first discussed in Strategy 13—may provide a solution. By buying an option to purchase the property, you will be able to give the owner the price he wants. If the property appreciates in value as anticipated, it will be well worth the agreed-upon price by the time you actually make the purchase. If the property's value fails to rise, you will, of course, be under no obligation to buy it, and will have lost only any option payments that have been made thus far.

The Strategy

To use this strategy, offer the price that the seller wants, but ask for a ten-year option and an option consideration that is 10 percent of the asking price. If you can't get a full ten-year option, try extending the option as you go along by offering amounts of money at various times. You might, for instance, offer the seller 5 percent of the asking price for a five-year option, and then, after that has passed, offer another 5 percent to extend the option for an additional five years.

Prior to exercising your option to buy the property, you will have plenty of time to plan how you will eventually put the real estate to use. You may even be able to arrange presales of land parcels—presales that can raise the cash for the final purchase. Then, when the time seems right, exercise your option by buying the property at the agreed-upon price.

A Scenario

A doctor was trying to sell a house he had owned for years and, according to residential salespeople, was asking a ridiculously high price. The doctor valued the house at $240,000, while it was probably worth only $150,000. However, the house was located across the street from a state-built home for senior citizens, and was only a block away from commercial zoning. These factors motivated the doctor to keep his price high, but did not motivate potential buyers to pay $90,000 above market value.

I convinced a client to buy a ten-year option on the doctor's home. The client put $25,000 down as option consideration at the asking price of $240,000. For ten years, he was to pay nothing else on the property while the owner paid the taxes and insurance, and maintained the building and grounds.

Five years later, in order to expand the senior citizens home, the state condemned the doctor's house, paying $750,000 for the property. At that point, my client exercised his option, and the doctor received $215,000 in keeping with the option agreement. My client, on the other hand, netted $510,000 on his original investment of $25,000.

Using a Created Mortgage to Finance a Purchase

You probably know that any property you own has value above and beyond any mortgage that may exist on it. In other words, it has *equity*, which can be defined as the difference between the fair market value of a property and the remaining money due on the mortgage. This equity is a frozen asset, though, meaning that it is not liquid and available for use. How can you unfreeze it? The strategy is simple. By creating a mortgage against your property, you can put your equity to work and use it to acquire other real estate and personal property.

The Strategy

Let's say that you own ten free-and-clear acres of land valued at $30,000. You don't wish to sell the land, but at the same time, you do need financing for a new real estate purchase.

Approach the owner of the property you want, and offer to exchange a note and first mortgage on your ten acres for an equal amount of equity in his land. Depending on the amount of the loan and the value of the property being bought, the paper may be traded for part or all of the down payment and purchase price. By circumventing banks and credit unions—paths normally taken to secure a mortgage—you will escape the payment of points, and will not have to comply with tight money regulations. In fact, you and the seller can tailor-make the mortgage by determining the mortgage rate, the amount and timing of payments, and all other terms and conditions.

Once you and the seller have agreed on the terms of the mortgage, have your attorney create the actual mortgage and note. When the transaction is closed, you will start making payments on the note. You will still own the land against which the note is secured, and will also own the second property. Moreover, the new purchase will have been made with no money down.

A Scenario

A client of mine decided to run for political office, and, feeling certain that he would win, chose to set up a property that would provide him with spendable income when he finally retired from the political field some ten years hence.

The two of us decided to use some free-and-clear land that was part of his farm as a means of providing a down payment for his new investment. According to recent sales in the area, the land had a solid value of $60,000, so we decided to create a first mortgage against the property in the amount of $30,000, payable over five years at 10-percent interest. Payments were to be made annually, as that best suited my client's income picture.

Soon, we found the perfect income property—an apartment house that could easily produce $1,500 per month in spendable income, and would therefore eventually solve some of my client's retirement problems. The building's owner gladly took the created mortgage as a down payment on the apartment building. The timing, we knew, was great. Because the mortgage would be paid off five years before my client's retirement, he would have a five-year period during which he would still be earning income, but would no longer being making payments on the mortgage.

Understanding Real Estate-Backed Paper

As you learned in Strategy 2, notes are one of the many types of property you can exchange for real estate. Just as important, notes can generate a steady flow of cash, enabling you to finance further real estate purchases. If you are not familiar with notes, it makes sense to spend some time now learning about them and discovering how they can help ensure adequate financing for a host of profitable real estate acquisitions.

What Is a Note?

Loans against real estate come in two parts. There's the security instrument, which may be a mortgage, deed of trust, or land sale contract; and the note. The *security instrument* pledges the property to the lender of the money as security for payment. The *note*—sometimes called a promissory note—is a legal document that obligates the borrower to repay the mortgage at a stated interest rate during a specified period of time. The note, then, is a promise to pay, and is what binds the borrower to the terms of the loan. The holder of the note—a bank, a mortgage company, or a private lender such as you—receives a regular series of payments as the borrower pays back both the principal and the interest over the term of the loan.

What Determines a Note's Value?

A number of things help determine a note's value. The first is the amount to be repaid. This, however, must be considered in light of the value of the property. A note with a lower loan-to-value ratio—in other words, a note in which the amount of money borrowed is small in relation to the property's value—is more desirable than a note with a higher ratio. In such a case, the borrower has greater equity in the property, and more incentive to pay back the loan.

A note's interest rate also plays a part in determining its value. The higher the rate, the greater the note's desirability.

The term of the loan—the period of time in which the debt has to be repaid—also has an impact on the note's value. Because of inflation and the concept of future value for present dollars, a note with a shorter term is generally more valuable than one with a longer term.

The price of the note is another variable that affects its value. Every note has a face value at its creation. For instance, if the loan is made for $10,000, the face value of that note at its creation is $10,000. But often, the original lender—a bank or mortgage company, for instance—later seeks to sell the note for immediate cash. While the lender may sell the note for the actual amount of principal that remains owed, more often, to attract buyers, it sells the note at a discount—that is, for less than its current balance. Clearly, the larger the *discount*—the difference between the face value of the note and the price paid for it—the more valuable the note is to the buyer.

How much can discount affect a note's yield? Let's return to our example of the $10,000 note, and further assume that the note is paying $100 a month, including principal and interest at the rate of 10 percent. If you were to buy that note at the various discount prices listed below, notice how your yield would differ.

Face Amount	Price Paid	Annual Yield
$10, 000	$9,000	11.69 %
$10, 000	$8,000	13.71 %
$10, 000	$7,000	16.19 %
$10, 000	$6,000	19.37 %
$10, 000	$5,000	23.64 %

Finally, it's important to understand that the time at which the note is actually paid off also affects its value. Sometimes, the borrower pays the note off earlier than expected. By shortening the term of the loan, this boosts the note's yield. This added value is sometimes called a *bonus-yield*.

How Do You Acquire Notes?

You can acquire notes in two basic ways. First, you can originate the note—meaning that you deal directly with the borrower and actually create the loan. This option allows you to negotiate the conditions so that the amount of the loan, the interest rate, and the length of the loan are a good match for your resources. It's not too difficult to find an opportunity to originate a loan. Prospects can be found by contacting local mortgage brokers, real estate companies, and builders and developers.

Your second option is to purchase an existing note. In such a case, you will have to accept existing terms. However, as discussed earlier, it is often possible to buy an existing note at a discount and enjoy a higher profit. It's a simple matter to locate notes that are for sale. First, try putting an ad in the newspaper. State that you wish to buy notes, and include your phone number. Also look for newspaper ads with the heading "Wanted to Buy" or "Want to Sell." Finally, write to real estate offices, escrow officers, bank loan officers, lawyers, and accountants—all of whom come in contact with sellers of paper. Very soon, you should find a good many notes coming your way.

Keeping and Trading Notes

Once you have bought a note, consider holding onto it and enjoying the payments as they stream in. After all, if you own a note that is yielding 10 to 35 percent a year, and you need cash flow, there is no reason to part with your investment. To make the note work even harder for you, use the cash flow to buy more notes or, better yet, to finance real estate purchases.

Another option is to trade the note. A good solid note is valuable property. I have exchanged notes for cars, airplanes, jewelry, horses, flying instructions, real estate classes, carpentry, and boats. And, of course, I have exchanged notes for real estate, including raw land, personal homes, and commercial buildings. Keep in mind that although you may have paid sixty cents on the dollar to buy the note, you can probably exchange it for its full face value. I know several brokers who pay their rent by getting face value for paper that they acquired at a discount.

As you buy more notes, generate more cash, and purchase more property, you can play a variety of "games." You can, for instance, sell one note for the cash you need to sweeten the note you are offering at face value to buy an investment property. Or you can use $100,000 worth of notes for which you paid $75,000 cash, to buy a house; turn around and get a $75,000 bank loan on the property, thus replacing your original capital; rent the property to make the payments; and use the loan money to buy more paper.

A "Note" of Caution

As you've learned, notes can generate high returns, and can also be used to barter and trade. Moreover, notes come in all sizes, and therefore are appropriate for all types of investors, large and small. However, it pays to be cautious.

First, if you are new to the world of notes, start by sticking to senior notes, sometimes called *firsts*—notes that have no liens before them; and to *seconds*—notes that have only one lien before them. Firsts are generally quite secure, because in the event that the borrower fails to make his payments, the person holding the senior note will be the first to receive the proceeds from any sale of the borrower's property. The holder of a second—a note in second payback position—is in a less secure position, as he will be second in line to receive payment in the event of default. However, in exchange for greater risk, the buyer receives greater returns.

Second, be sure to use a qualified attorney to draw up the document when originating a note, and to review the terms of any note that you're buying. Especially if the note is not straightforward, you'll need your attorney to translate the legalese and identify any clauses that may later cause problems. As long as you proceed with caution and use expert legal advice, the notes you purchase are sure to boost your ability to finance profitable real estate investments.

Buying Property for 20 Percent Off While Paying the Asking Price

The inset on page 57 explained that in the absence of ready cash, real estate-backed notes can be traded for property. This strategy adds a twist to the earlier concept, and will actually allow you to meet the seller's price while getting a 20-percent discount.

The Strategy

Let's say that you find a piece of property that you want, and during negotiations, the seller states that he can help finance the transaction by carrying back some or all of the purchase price on a note and mortgage. You, however, can handle the purchase with the cash you have and bank financing.

Negotiate the transaction with the seller, discussing the down payment, the size of the note, the interest rate, and the term of the loan. Then insert a clause in the purchase agreement, stating that he will accept a note and mortgage not for the property being purchased, but for *another* property.

Once you have reached an agreement, search for paper that you can buy at a discount, using your remaining cash. (See page 59 for information on buying notes.) When you find suitable paper, make an offer that will give you a yield of between 10 and 20 percent. Remember that, as discussed in the earlier inset, the steeper the discount offered on the paper, the greater the yield will be.

Until the seller of the property agrees to accept your note, place an option on the paper rather than making an outright purchase. Once you get the seller's approval, consummate the purchase of the paper. Then, describing it as "Exhibit A," make the paper part of the purchase agreement at the closing.

A Scenario

A young realtor friend wanted to purchase an eight-plex whose owner was willing to accept some cash plus *soft paper* on other property—paper with lower-than-market interest rates and long-term payments. My friend came to me seeking existing paper he could purchase at a discount. I didn't have any, but suggested that he make an offer that would include both cash and paper.

Together, my friend and I structured an offer than included some free-and-clear lots at appraised value, some paper paying interest of 10 percent or more, and some cash. The offer was accepted.

Next, we looked for existing paper paying at least 10-percent interest. The paper would have to be in first or second position, and on acceptable property. We found a subdivider who had a lot of paper paying from 9- to 14-percent interest—all seconds after a land improvement loan with a local bank. Land sales had been very slow for the past two years, and the subdivider was hurting. We offered to buy $150,000 worth of his paper for $90,000 cash, provided that our eight-plex seller would accept the paper.

The eight-plex owner accepted the paper, and we closed the purchase of the paper at the same time we closed the purchase of the eight-plex. For the $300,000 eight-plex, we paid $75,000 in cash; $150,000 in paper; and $75,000 in free-and-clear lots. By paying only $90,000 for the $150,000 paper, we saved $60,000—20 percent of the purchase price.

Paying Your Closing Costs With Notes

When property is purchased through a realtor, the brokerage fee usually amounts to 5 to 10 percent of the total price. Add in your other closing costs—discount points, title insurance premiums, inspection and appraisal fees, and attorney's fees, to name just a few—and you may be paying the equivalent of many down payments over and above the actual price of the property. When financing is difficult, these fees can hinder you from acquiring the property you want. A great solution is to offer to pay for these items in notes instead of cash. Often, this strategy can overcome obstacles caused by a cash shortfall, and allow you to close the deal.

The Strategy

You are about to close on a transaction, and have found that the closing fees will eat up all of your cash reserves. Instead of financially weakening yourself, negotiate to pay each of the various closing costs with a separate note. This will allow you to pay the closing costs over time, rather than all at once. In a sense, you will be using other people's money to complete the purchase. As a result, you will preserve your cash position and emerge with greater financial strength.

A Scenario

I had worked long and hard to find an income property that would suit the needs of one of my long-time clients. As we approached the closing, we realized that his closing costs would total nearly $60,000. At this point, my client surprised me by asking that we arrange several notes so he could pay the fees over time, rather than in a single blow. It took a period of negotiation, but eventually, everyone involved agreed to accept notes for the money due them, and the transaction closed.

Deal-Making Strategy
Using a Life Estate to Obtain the Property You Want

A *life estate* is an agreement whereby the owner of a piece of property transfers title to another individual or to an organization, while retaining the right to occupy and otherwise enjoy full use of the property for either a term of years or the lifetime of one or more individuals. A life estate can be granted to a single person, a couple, or a family. Generally, though, it is granted to elderly people because of the likelihood that their lifetime will not exceed the value of the agreement. The elderly people benefit by being able to live on the property without paying any costs other than utilities.

Certainly, not every person, elderly or otherwise, wants or needs a life estate. In some cases, though, a life estate is just what a property owner is looking for, and can give you the means to acquire the real estate you want.

The Strategy

Let's assume that you have found a piece of property that is occupied by an elderly couple, and is underutilized in the sense that it is zoned for apartments, condos, or commercial use. You know that if the property were yours, you could turn it into a highly profitable investment. Let's further assume that you own another property—a small rental house—and can offer the couple a life estate in that property in exchange for their current home.

Before making an offer, use actuarial tables—available from a life insurance company—to predict how long the couple might occupy your property. This will enable you to determine your cost in making the life estate offer. Simply multiply the monthly rent on your house by the number of months of the couple's projected remaining life to calculate the price of the property you are offering. Don't forget that the value of any future dollars you will be paying is less than the value of today's dollars, so the actual amount should be discounted by 30 to 40 percent. Your objective is to provide them with housing that will cost them nothing except utilities, but will not cause you to go bankrupt in the process.

If the cost of the life estate is reasonable, you can then make an offer to the couple. When doing so, be sure to explain to them and any of their advisors—children, attorneys, and friends—that they will have to pay no taxes, no insurance, and no maintenance or repairs. They need pay only utilities to live comfortably in their new home.

A Scenario

A developer was searching for commercial land on which to construct an office building. He soon found a plot that seemed perfect for the project. The only problem was that the house cited on the land was inhabited by an elderly couple who refused to sell their property.

Not one to give up easily, the developer talked to the couple and soon found that they were not entirely happy with their situation. The house had become too much for them to handle. They were having difficulty paying the increased taxes and handling the utility bills for a structure built before modern plumbing, insulation, and lighting fixture. Repairs were eating into their already tight budget. What they wanted was a roof over their heads that would be maintained for them, without cost or worry, for the rest of their lives.

The developer felt he had a solution both to his problem and theirs. He owned a duplex—not a new duplex, but one that he felt might appeal to the couple in that it was a single story and was located close to their grocery store, library, and church. The developer had taken rapid depreciation on the duplex and had a low cost basis in it, which meant that any sale would result in his losing a large part of his equity to capital gains taxes. He knew that exchanging a life estate in half of the duplex and renting the other half would provide enough income to pay the property's remaining debt. And, of course, it would enable him to proceed with the office building project.

The developer engaged an attorney to write up a life estate document, and closed the transaction two days before the builder broke ground on the office building development.

Five years later, the husband died and the widow wanted out of the duplex. The builder, being in a better cash position at that time, bought out the widow's life estate, and she moved in with her daughter. At the right time and the right place, the life estate had solved everyone's problems.

Combining a Purchase With a Lease

S ometimes you find the exact piece of property you want—real estate that will provide investment growth for your income, or make the perfect home for your new business. The only problem is that the cost is too high. In a case such as this, a simple solution is often the answer. By purchasing the building only and renting the land on which it's sited, you can make that investment or start that business without draining your financial resources.

The Strategy

You have found a great building for your new business. The location, the size—everything is just what you wanted. The only problem is that you can't afford the asking price, and the seller has no intention of accepting less. You wish there was some way of getting the building you want at a price you can afford.

Approach the buyer and offer to buy the building only, and rent the land. If you are working with a real estate broker, he should be able to guide you in coming up with a realistic offer—one based on the market price of the building. If you are working alone, some detective work will be necessary. The value of a comparable plot of raw land can usually be determined by examining the real estate booklets you find on supermarket racks, or by contacting local realtors. Once you've placed a value on the land, you can easily subtract that cost from the seller's asking price, and arrive at a ballpark figure for the building alone.

Even if the seller has been eager to dispose of the entire piece of property, he is likely to see the benefit of holding onto the land and enjoying a safe long-term cash flow. The land will probably appreciate over the years, producing an increase in value as well as increased land lease payments. The benefits to you, the buyer and tenant, are just as clear. You will be able to get the building you want at a price you can afford. Moreover, all of your lease payments will be fully deductible as a business expense, giving you a nice write-off each and every year of the lease.

One last word is in order. Financing is sometimes a problem in a situation such as this. Most lenders, though, are now willing to make a loan by using the building only as security.

A Scenario

A few years ago, a client of mine was looking for an industrial property with a large combination office-warehouse. We found a listing for such a property, but the asking price—$1,200,000— was well above what my client could afford. Moreover, when we contacted the realtor who represented the owner, we learned that the owner had a high opinion of his property's value, and no intention of accepting a lower bid. In fact, the property had been for sale for some time, and the owner had rejected a number of offers because they were too low.

The owner's broker and I met for coffee the next day to see if we could work out a deal that would be acceptable to both parties. It seemed that his client wanted to retire, and one of the reasons he was stalling for a high price was that he expected to retire on the proceeds of the sale. We therefore came up with a plan whereby my client would offer to purchase the building for $700,000, and would lease the land for fifty years at 6 percent of the land's market value, or $30,000 a year. The purchase, of course, would give the seller immediate money, while the lease would provide him with a nice monthly payment to augment his retirement income. Both clients agreed to the terms, and the deal was closed.

Converting Principal Payments Into Tax-Deductible Lease Payments

Even real estate investors new to the field know that while the interest portion of a mortgage payment is tax-deductible, the principal is not. This strategy is designed for buyers who are looking for a bigger tax write-off than that provided by a standard purchase. By combining a standard down payment with lease payments—which are a 100-percent deductible business expense—it maximizes tax benefits while providing the buyer with the property he wants. At the same time, this strategy provides the seller with the same cash he would make on a traditional sale.

The Strategy

You have found a building that would be the perfect home for your growing business. You have sufficient cash for the down payment, and can easily make the monthly mortgage payments. However, at this point, you know that your business would benefit from greater tax write-offs than would result from a traditional purchase.

Approach the owner of the property, and offer to purchase the property in a somewhat untraditional way. You will give the owner the same down payment that he would receive in a conventional sale, but it will now be called a lease consideration. The two of you will then arrange for a ten- to thirty-year lease, which will enable you to make the same monthly payments that you would have made on a mortgage. He, however, will not have to wait for his money, as he will sell the lease to the bank, immediately getting the remainder of his asking price.

During the term of the lease, you will make lease payments to the bank. At the end of that period, you will pay an additional $100, and per the lease agreement, the property's title will pass to you. You will not have paid any more than you would have paid in a standard purchase. For the term of the lease, though, you will have been able to write off the full amount of every monthly lease payment, in effect, writing off both the substituted principal and interest.

A Scenario

One of my clients needed a building for his business, and we soon found a property that was a good match for both his needs and his resources. The asking price for the building was $1,000,000. My client had $400,000 in cash for the down payment, and found a bank willing to loan him $600,000 at 9-percent interest. With all his financing in place, we intended to close the sale in thirty days.

As always, I ran the numbers for my client, including his tax position in ownership. When he finished reading my analysis, I could see that he wasn't happy. His company was making a lot of money and paying a lot of taxes. He wondered if he could get further tax benefits from the property.

Instead of arranging an outright purchase, we structured a lease on the building for ten years at $103,300 a year. The seller then sold the lease to the bank for $600,000 cash. My client gave the seller the $400,000 he would have ordinarily given him as a down payment. This payment was received by the seller as a lease consideration, and contributed to the overall payments my client was making to secure the use of the property. The seller, then, received his asking price of $1,000,000—$400,000 from my client and $600,000 from the bank for the sale of the lease. And the bank got a solid ten-year lease with interest on its loaned money.

My client now has a $1,000,000 building. Each year, he writes off the $103,300 of lease payments and a tenth of the lease consideration payment. At the end of the lease, according to the agreement, my client will make a buyout payment of $100, and the title will pass to him.

Understanding the Land Lease

Land lease is a rental agreement that allows a nonowner to use land in a manner acceptable to both parties. The land lease can be used in different ways under different circumstances. In Strategy 19, for instance, the investor buys the building on a property, but—to keep costs down—only leases the land on which the building is sited. In Strategy 21, the investor leases raw land in order to construct new buildings. In both cases, the investor saves money by leasing rather than purchasing the land.

When you take possession of property through a land lease, you pay rent, and may improve the land through the addition of new structures, as long as both parties have agreed to such additions. At the end of the lease, the entire property—including any improvements made in the form of houses, shopping centers, etc.—reverts to the owner. Most agreements stipulate that upon expiration of the lease, the tenant will restore the land to the condition it was in when first leased. If and when the tenant makes an improvement that the owner wishes to keep, however, this provision is often changed at the end of the lease. Land being rented for new construction is generally leased for thirty to ninety-nine years.

Because of the many benefits of the land lease, this agreement is used increasingly by sophisticated real estate investors. First, the person who rents the land—the lessee—does not have to pay for the land, making this an attractive option for investors who are low in capital. He can write the lease payments off his income as an expense item, which he could not do if he were buying the land. He can also include the value of the land in the overall value of his project, and can obtain a loan by using the *leasehold*—the estate on which the tenant has the lease—as collateral.

The owner of the land also realizes several advantages. The monthly payments he receives through a land lease eventually bring him more money than he would receive through a sale of the same land. The land also remains in his estate to pass on to his heirs, and continues to increase in value through appreciation. If and when a new building is constructed on his property, he has good security, provided that the financing is structured so that it does not threaten his ownership in the event of a default by the tenant. Moreover, the lessor does not pay capital gains tax as he would on a sale; he keeps title to the land; and eventually, if desired, he acquires any improvements made on his property.

Using a Land Lease to Build

S trategy 19 demonstrated that you can sometimes finance the purchase of improved property by buying the building only, and leasing the land on which it's sited. But that's not the only use of a land lease agreement. This strategy shows how you can obtain use of raw land through a land lease, build on the land, and use the newly created structures as you wish for the duration of the lease. Whether you're planning to construct an apartment building or an office for your own business, land lease can often enable you to build when a dearth of capital would otherwise make the project impossible.

The Strategy

You have found a piece of raw land that would be the perfect site for your new office building. Unfortunately, you simply don't have the cash on hand for a down payment.

Approach the owner of the property and offer to rent the land for an agreed-upon term. During the term of the lease, you will make monthly rent payments to the property owner. In return, you will be allowed to build upon the leased land and to use the newly created structures as you see fit. At the termination of the lease, the property, including your office building, will revert to the owner.

The immediate advantage of the land lease to you, the lessee, is clear. You will be able to use the land without buying it. But this arrangement will provide another advantage as well, because your rent payments will be a fully deductible business expense. Meanwhile, the owner of the property will benefit from a constant stream of income for the term of the lease. (For more information on the land lease, see the inset on page 74.)

It's important to note that the land lease isn't useful only when you lack the capital needed to purchase the land. It is also useful when the owner of the land is not willing to sell, but *is* willing to enter into a long-term lease.

A Scenario

A client of mine was operating his business out of a relatively small office building, which he owned. The business was growing by leaps and bounds, however, and he needed to build not only new office space, but also a large warehouse. He felt that the plot of land for sale adjacent to his business would be a great site, as it would provide room not only for his current construction plans, but also for any future needs. He asked me to look into it.

I contacted the realtor who represented the owner of the neighboring property, and discovered that the asking price was $150,000. Unfortunately, this was too steep for my client. After discussing the situation, my client and I came up with another proposal. We offered to pay the owner $1,200 a month to lease his land. The lease would run for ninety-nine years, and would permit no new financing on the property without the owner's consent. And, of course, it would allow my client to build the structures necessary for the expansion of his business.

After some negotiation, the owner accepted the offer, and my client began making lease payments. He is now enjoying use of the land without investing substantial capital, and the land owner is enjoying monthly income that will increase annually with the cost of living index.

Obtaining 100-Percent Financing Through Sale and Leaseback

S ometimes an investor owns a piece of property, but needs a high percentage of financing to proceed with its development. He requires the income that the project will eventually provide, but can't get to that point without additional cash. In the meantime—especially in a fluctuating interest market—conventional lenders may be unwilling to give him a long-term loan.

What's the solution? In such a situation, the investor can often get his financing through *leaseback*—an arrangement whereby a piece of property is simultaneously sold and leased back to the seller, usually for long-term use.

The Strategy

You are the owner of a piece of raw land that you wish to develop, but to do so, you need a high percentage of financing. With your development plans in hand, sell the land to a lender, private or bank, agreeing to lease it back. Then apply for a bank loan to finance the improvements—buildings, paving, landscaping, roads, etc. Generally, you will get 100 percent of the land value in your sale to the lender, and 75 percent of the value of the improvements through the loan.

If you have an improved property—say, a shopping center—which requires financing for further development, sell the *land only* to a lending institution such as a bank, and then lease it back. This will allow you to retain your equity in the buildings located on the leased land. Then acquire a bank loan to finance the improvements needed. Again, you will probably be able to borrow 75 percent of the value of the improvements, and will also have the cash from the land sale.

Regardless of which of the above strategies you use, you will get a high percentage of financing. You will also enjoy cash flow, rent increases, and management and maintenance income.

It should be noted that the leaseback is also useful when you need cash for *other* ventures—for the buying of new property, for instance. In fact, whenever your chief goal is to get cash, the leaseback should be considered.

A Scenario

A developer owned a parcel of land that he had purchased five years before. He still owed $150,000 on the property, but had plans to build a shopping center and 200 apartments.

Although the developer was ready to begin building, his cash was tied up in other projects. At the same time, a lender was interested in financing the construction, but was worried about fluctuations in the interest market.

The developer sold the land to the lender for fair market value, which gave the developer a nice profit. He then leased the land from the lender for sixty-eight years. The lease included a cost-of-living clause, which allowed the lender to make annual adjustments in the lease payments based on the Department of Labor's cost of living index. The lease also stipulated that once the structures has been completed, the developer would pay 2 percent of the gross rents to the lender.

The bank then loaned the developer 75 percent of the cost of constructing the improvements. With the money from the land sale and the 75-percent loan, the developer had enough cash to complete construction with no other capital.

Using the Velvet Hammer in Leaseback Situations

In Strategy 22, you learned how you can obtain financing through leaseback—through simultaneously selling a piece of your property and leasing it back. The benefits of this strategy are clear. Through leaseback, you—the seller—can get the cash you need to develop that same piece of land, to buy another property, or to make other real estate investments.

But let's turn this situation around for a moment and see it from the perspective of the buyer. Why? Because if you are a real estate investor, eventually, you may decide to buy property and lease it back to the original owner. After all, this strategy has benefits for the buyer as well as the seller, as it provides him with a management-free income-producing investment. It's worth noting, though, that as the buyer in a leaseback situation, you have to be cautious. The original owner may reneg on his promise to lease the property and provide the management you need to benefit from your real estate acquisition. What can you do if the original owner fails to perform as promised? That's where the "velvet hammer" comes in.

When the purchase is made, require the seller to carry back some of the financing, which you, the buyer, will pay a portion of each month. Then, within your lease agreement insert a clause stating that if the seller defaults on the leaseback—if he does not perform according to the terms of the agreement—a specified amount will be deducted from the money that is yet to be paid him on the purchase. In actuality, of course, a number of steps would have to be taken before that money could be deducted. If the seller does not agree in writing that he has defaulted, you might have to go to court. However, a good velvet hammer clause states that if the matter goes to court, the loser will have to pay attorney's fees and court costs for the winner. Such a clause, then, would provide a great deal of motivation for the seller to keep his promise, making your new property a much more secure investment.

Combining a Lease With a Third-Party Investor

As you learned in Strategy 20, by leasing the property you want from the owner, you can obtain use of the property, as well as a great tax write-off from fully deductible lease payments. But what if the owner isn't interested in leasing his property, but only wants to make a sale? This strategy combines a lease with a third-party investor to get you use of that great real estate without draining your finances. And, just as in Strategy 20, it allows you to ultimately buy the property you want.

The Strategy

You have found a vacant building for sale, and while it isn't exactly what you want for your business, you know that it can be remodeled to suit your needs. The problem is that the owner isn't interested in leasing the property, much less remodeling it. His goal is to sell the building for immediate cash, and you're in no position to make the purchase.

Find an investor who is looking for appreciation, cash flow, and depreciation benefits, and ask him to buy and remodel the building, with the guarantee that you will rent it from him on a long-term basis. (See the inset "Finding Coinvestors and Partners" on page 101 for tips on locating an investor.) Be prepared to draft a written agreement that states the term of the lease and the amount of the monthly rent payments. The investor has to know that he has a tenant who is ready, willing, and able to make this property an income producer.

If you are interested in eventually owning the property, instead of using a regular lease, draft a *lease with option to purchase*—a lease that gives you the right to purchase the property at an agreed-upon price after having paid rent for a specified period of time. By the time the lease has expired, you may be in a better position to make the down payment required for the purchase. The agreement can even be structured so that either all of the rent or a portion of the rent is credited towards the sales price.

A Scenario

A young man came into my office one day in response to my listing of a vacant building. He was relatively new to his business, but his franchise company was pressuring him to open a second restaurant. He did not have enough capital to purchase and remodel the vacant building, but was convinced that this was the perfect property for his franchise. He therefore was interested in a lease. The problem? The property owner had no desire to lease.

Working together, the young man and I drafted a lease contract whereby he would agree to lease the remodeled property for ten years, with two ten-year options to renew, for $3,000 a month. Because the young man hoped to someday own the building, the lease also included an option to purchase. This option, however, could be exercised only after he had rented the property for at least ten years.

I called a local investor and described the building that was up for sale. Would the investor be interested in buying and remodeling the property if he had a guaranteed tenant? He would.

I then worked with the franchisee and the investor, modifying the terms of the lease as necessary. With the help of a bank loan, the investor was soon able to begin remodeling the property, and four months later, the young man moved his new equipment into the building and opened his second franchise.

Acting as Buyer and Future Tenant

n Strategy 23, you discovered that when you want to lease a property which is available only for sale, you can often find an investor willing to buy the property and remodel it for a guaranteed tenant. But let's say that you can find no investor who's willing or able to make an outright purchase of the land you want. Wouldn't it be great if you could secure a would-be buyer and arrange the financing for him, thereby creating the situation that you want? Well, you can. By acting as both buyer and future tenant, you can put the property in the hands of a willing owner, and actually specify the terms and conditions of the lease, thereby providing yourself with the land you need at terms you can live with.

The Strategy

You have found a piece of raw land that would be a perfect site for your new office building. Unfortunately, the land is for sale at a price that's way beyond your means, and no bank or private party loan is available on unimproved land at this time. Moreover, while the property owner is willing to lease the land, his terms are in no way acceptable to you.

First, arrange to buy the land from the owner for the asking price. The purchase will not happen right away, but will wait until the financing is in place.

Now, pretend that you own the land, and write a lease for yourself as lessee (tenant) that stipulates the exact terms and conditions for which you're looking. True, the land is still in the hands of the original owner, but your next step will move towards finding a new owner who will accept the terms you want.

You now want to find a house for sale with an asking price that's higher than the price of the raw land. Ideally, the house will have been on the market for quite a while, and the owner will be motivated to sell. When you find the right property, offer to trade the raw land with the lease for the house. The homeowner, in other words, will exchange his house not only for ownership of the land, but also for a guaranteed income stream from you, the tenant.

The owner of the land is, of course, not looking for a house, but for cash. So at this point, arrange for a conventional mortgage on the house for the price of the raw land, using the house as security for the loan. The borrowed money will be used to purchase the raw land from the owner.

Once all of these arrangements have been finalized, the transactions will be made simultaneously, with each contingent upon the other. The owner of the raw land will get his asking price; the raw land and lease will be acquired by the homeowner; and you will get your lease, as well as the house. Ultimately, you can sell the house, and use any profit you enjoy to develop the raw land according to the terms of your new lease.

A Scenario

A corporation owned a corner lot that was advertised "For sale, lease, or build to suit." My client responded to the ad, and found that the owners wanted to sell the land for $300,000, or to rent it for only a short period of time. My client had neither the capital to buy, nor the interest in a short-term lease.

My client and I wrote a long-term lease that reflected the value of the land, and would allow him to construct the building he needed for his business. We then started looking for a free-and-clear house that was up for sale. Soon, we found a retired general—a widower—who was thinking of leaving the state. Fortunately for us, he was not interested in a lump sum payment, but instead wanted additional cash flow to augment his retirement income. He was therefore eager to trade his house, equity for equity, for ownership of the land, as well as a lease that would provide him with regular monthly payments.

The house had been appraised at $375,000, which made it easy to get an 80-percent mortgage in the amount of $300,000. This money was used to pay the owner of the vacant land. As soon as the payment had been made, the land became the property of my client, who immediately traded it for the house.

The client sold the house for $347,500 to a party who assumed the new loan of $300,000. After paying the realtor's fee and closing costs, my client found he had enough cash left to pay his rent for a few months while he put together the plans for his new office building.

Maximizing the Income From Income Property

Many of the strategies in this book explain how you can use property you already own to finance a new real estate venture. Sometimes the property is used as security for a loan. Sometimes it's sold. And sometimes it's leased.

Strategy 25 also uses real estate holdings to generate cash. This time, though, a combination of a sale and a lease help you maximize cash flow, yet maintain control of the property and even preserve some of your equity.

The Strategy

Let's say that you own an apartment building that is generating a reasonable cash flow. You need cash to buy another income-producing property, but you don't have adequate equity in the current property to secure a loan for the amount of cash you need.

First, determine the cash value of the land on which your apartment house stands. Now subtract the value of the land and any money still owed on the property from the total value of the property. This will give you the equity you now have in the apartment building itself. (Total property value minus value of land and mortgage equals equity in apartment.)

Now sell 80 percent of the equity you have in the building, retaining 20 percent of the equity, as well as the management contract, maintenance contract, and control of the property. The buyer will, of course, get 80 percent of the income from the apartment house, based on the equity of the building only. You will get immediate cash from the sale, as well as a steady cash flow from your remaining equity and from the two contracts.

You still have complete ownership of what is now a free-and-clear parcel of land. This means that you have two ways to squeeze still more cash out of your property. You can sell the land lease, which will give you immediate cash and provide the buyer with monthly income; or you can use the land to secure a loan—a strategy that will also give you an immediate infusion of cash.

A Scenario

One of my friends owned an old hotel that had been converted into low-cost housing for elderly people. The property was valued at $240,000 with a loan of $160,000, leaving $80,000 equity. An active real estate investor, my friend wanted to get as large a cash flow as possible from his project. He therefore did the following:

1. He valued the land at $30,000 and leased it for a 12-percent return, or $3,600 a year, with increases due to inflation and taxes. The lease was a *net lease*—a lease in which the tenants pay taxes, insurance, and maintenance—so my friend had to pay no expenses. His income, however, would go up as tax assessments or inflation increased the rent.

2. He sold 80 percent of the remaining equity for $40,000, and guaranteed the investor a 6-percent cash flow before he took anything for his remaining 20-percent equity position.

3. He retained management of the building, which grossed him $14,400 per year.

4. He also kept the maintenance and cleaning contracts on the building, which grossed him another $3,000 per year.

When the transactions were complete, my friend had received $40,000 in cash, while retaining the land for sale or holding purposes; picked up $17,400 in supplementary contracts; and got whatever benefits in appreciation, principal reduction, and cash flow accrued to his 20-percent equity position. He also enjoyed the depreciation associated with owning improved property.

Using Sale or Exchange and Buyback

S trategy 22 showed how you can obtain financing through leaseback. Yet another way to get the funding you need is to sell a piece of your property and then buy it back, or to exchange your property for another and then buy it back. While both of these strategies require the expert help of your attorney and your accountant, when done properly, they can greatly benefit not only you but also the investor who purchases the property from you.

The Strategy

Let's assume that you own a piece of raw land and you want to put a building on it, but you lack the necessary funds. To use this strategy, first sell the property to another investor for its current market value. Then, after that transaction has closed, enter into an agreement to buy the land back at a higher price, using a small down payment, with the new seller financing the purchase by carrying back the note and mortgage.

The transaction will meet your goal of generating the immediate cash you need to improve your property. But the other investor will also benefit, as he will make a profit when he sells the land back to you at a higher price. And by carrying back the note, he will get a higher return than he would if he left his money sitting in the bank.

To effect an exchange and buyback, make an offer to exchange your property for another piece of real estate that you want to own. Once the exchange has been effected, just as in the sale and buyback, you can enter into an agreement to buy the original property back at a higher price.

Both of these transactions require the advice and counsel of experienced lawyers and tax accountants who specialize in real estate. Whether the first transaction is a sale or an exchange, the buyback agreement should be verbal—a gentleman's agreement—rather than a written document. If written, it could be scrutinized by the Internal Revenue Service and later declared a loan, which would upset the new depreciation schedule. Moreover, the property must be repurchased by a legal entity different from the one that originally owned it—a different corporation or limited partnership, for example. Generally speaking, if the seller is a different entity from the repurchaser, there is no written promise to repurchase the property, and there is a time lag between the sale and the repurchase, the transaction will go unquestioned. If you have three to nine months of time before using this strategy, submit a letter to the IRS in which you explain the circumstances and detail your proposed course of action. The IRS will respond with a ruling that, if it's in your favor, will insure an ironclad transaction.

A Scenario

A client of mine—a professional man—owned the building that housed his business. The building was valued at $100,000, with a loan of $25,000 against it. Because he needed to raise at least $50,000 for another real estate venture, he asked me to help him sell his property as a means of raising cash. I quickly saw that he did not want to lose his building; he merely needed financing. So instead of a straightforward sale, I suggested a sale and buyback.

I obtained a loan commitment for him of $60,000 on the property, and procured a buyer willing to pay $90,000 cash with a $30,000 down payment. With the $30,000 down payment and

$35,000 net from the loan, less broker's fees and loan costs, my client ended up with about $58,000 to use in his new real estate investment.

After the first of the month, my client bought the building back in the name of a newly formed corporation. He paid $95,000 in the repurchase, which gave the seller a profit of $5,000. His new corporation started a new depreciation schedule based on the new price. The investor who bought his building and then sold it back to him earned an immediate profit on his purchase and sale. And by carrying back the note and mortgage, the investor created for himself a steady income stream for the term of the loan.

Using a Blanket Mortgage to Obtain Financing

As any real estate investor knows, all real property has equity—value that the owner has in the property over and above any existing debt. When you need financing, you can use a mortgage to borrow against that equity, thereby raising immediate cash. Sometimes, though, no single property can raise the amount of cash you need to finance a new venture. The solution? An effective strategy is to use a *blanket mortgage*—a single mortgage that covers more than one piece of real estate. This will enable you to get more cash than you could on any one property, and probably more than you could if you mortgaged each property individually.

The Strategy

You need financing for the development of a piece of property you bought a year ago. Because you still have relatively little equity in the property, you are unable to get a sufficiently large loan using only that real estate as security. Fortunately, though, you own another piece of property in the same town.

Approach a lender, and offer both properties as security for the loan. Note that you don't even have to own all the properties covered by the mortgage as long as the owners of the real estate are willing to lend them to you for the purpose of getting the loan.

Family members, for instance, may allow you to use their property as additional security for your blanket mortgage. Once the lender sees that the mortgage amount is adequately secured, you will be able to close the transaction.

The blanket mortgage is most easily obtained when the various properties are in the same city or county, but when a bank is the lender, the mortgage will work as long as all of the real estate is within the lending jurisdiction of the bank. If you are using a private lender, the properties just have to be verifiable.

A Scenario

A client was trying to raise $16,000 to finish the remodeling of a sixteen-unit apartment house that he had started before he ran out of money. The conventional lender declined to let him borrow further money, so he had to find another way to get the financing he needed, or risk losing the building.

My client approached a private lender, but couldn't interest him in making the loan. The lender simply didn't feel that the apartment house offered sufficient security in its uncompleted state. My client then asked if he would consider making the loan if additional security was provided in the form of a free-and-clear five-acre parcel on which was sited a trailer house. The lender agreed, and a single note was drawn showing that my client owed $16,000 to the lender. A mortgage was then created to cover the two properties, and my client got the money he needed to remodel his apartment house.

Using a Wraparound Mortgage to Secure New Financing

Everyone from the average homeowner to the savvy investor knows that when interest rates are low, a smart way to raise the funds you need is to place a mortgage on property you already own. But how about when mortgage rates are high? In those circumstances, is it possible to borrow against your property without having interest rates eat up your income?

If your property is already mortgaged and the interest rate on the existing mortgage is low, a wraparound mortgage presents a great solution. A *wraparound mortgage* combines an existing mortgage with a new loan, resulting in an interest rate that is somewhere between the old rate and the current market rate.

The Strategy

Let's say that you own a house on which there is a relatively low-interest loan. When you find that you need money to finance a real estate venture, you immediately think of placing a second mortgage on your home. The only problem is that the current mortgage rate is double the rate of your old mortgage.

Call your lender—conventional or private—and arrange for a wraparound mortgage. As already explained, the new mortgage will include the unpaid balance of the first one, and will bear an interest rate considerably less than the going rate because of the leverage on the existing loan. The new interest rate will actually be computed so that the new lender can make the market interest rate on only the money he funded, plus a small override on the existing loan—say, half of 1 percent. You will make one payment on both loans to the wraparound lender, who in turn will make payments on the original senior mortgage. And you will get the cash you need for your new investment.

A Scenario

A client of mine needed money to finance the building of a motel. Eleven years before, he had purchased a sixteen-unit apartment house on which he had an 8-percent mortgage. The remaining balance on the loan was $200,000, and he had $200,000 equity in the property.

The client wanted to obtain $100,000 by placing a second mortgage on his apartment house. However, the current interest rate of 12 percent was quite steep.

Fortunately, another client was looking for an investment, and offered the first client a wraparound mortgage. The lender took over the 8-percent loan and funded the borrower the additional $100,000 at an overall interest rate of 10.75—1.25 percent below the current market rate.

Finding Coinvestors and Partners

A coinvestor or partner can increase your investment power, enabling you to purchase properties that would otherwise be beyond your reach. If you are new to the world of investing, or if you have always made your investments solo, you may be wondering how you can go about finding appropriate people to help you finance some of your more ambitious ventures. Whether you're looking for a single investor to bring in some much-needed cash or you're searching for several investors to form a limited liability company or corporation, the goal is pretty much the same—to find people who not only have the money you need, but are also honest and trustworthy, and can work with you in a cooperative and harmonious manner.

To begin your search, use networking to discover if family, friends, or friends of friends may be interested in joining you. Clearly, people you already know and trust can make ideal partners, assuming that they have the requisite funds.

Don't overlook the various professionals who may have helped and advised you throughout your various real estate ventures. If you have successfully worked for many years with an experienced real estate agent or a savvy accountant, and you have confidence in the individual, consider offering him the new role of coinvestor. A partner with knowledge of the field of real estate or finance can be only a boon as you pursue both this and future projects.

If you fail to find a partner among the people you already know, try placing an ad in a newspaper, requesting that interested investors contact you. The people who are most likely to respond, of course, are those with high incomes—doctors, attorneys, engineers, and accountants, for instance. Many high-income professionals have private investment plans that they contribute to monthly, and are always looking for ventures that promise good returns. You'll want to screen each candidate carefully, though, to make sure that you'll be working with someone in whom you have trust. In addition to an in-depth interview, it's a wise move to check public records for the individual's participation in lawsuits. If there has been one in the last ten years, consider it a red flag, and ask your candidate for details before letting him buy in. There is no shortage of potential investors out there, so don't feel pressured to team up with the first person who comes along.

While you're searching for investors, keep the property tied up with an option or a purchase agreement. This will not only lock in the price, but will also prevent someone else—including anyone with whom you've discussed the investment—from snapping up the property before you've assembled your team.

Finally, structure the transaction so that you can maintain control of the property after the purchase. If you are forming a limited partnership, for instance, you'll want to maintain the position of general partner. (For information on limited partnerships and other types of syndications, see the inset on page 111.) If you're forming a corporation, the position of president will allow you to control the company's holdings. In other cases, you'll need to own a majority of the interests in the real estate. Only then will you be able to guide your project as you see fit, and reap rewards for both yourself and your coinvestors.

Financing Financed Raw Land

As many real estate investors know, raw land can eat up cash, leaving few resources for development. But there is a solution to this common problem. By finding an investor with heavy cash flow, you can infuse the project with needed financing, proceed with the development of the land, and even retain a good percentage of the equity.

The Strategy

Picture for a moment that you have purchased a parcel of land for future use. Unfortunately, you don't have the cash to finance development, and due to tight money, getting a construction loan is out of the question. In the meantime, because of the scarcity of construction and development money, the market for this land has softened so much that the value is less than is owed on the property. Because the land eats up more cash every month, you can't hold onto it, but you can't sell below your loans, either. Yet you know that the property will have real value when the economy experiences an upswing. Your goal is to get out of the negative cash flow position that has you in a bind, but to retain some of your equity.

If you are reasonably sure that the property will appreciate and will be highly usable in the future, find an investor with a high cash flow to come in and carry the payments until the land is developed. In return, give the investor a percentage of the equity—perhaps 49 percent. When construction begins, consider having the investor lend his financial statement to the project to acquire a better loan.

Both you and the new investor will benefit from this arrangement. You will be able to keep the growth land even though the market is temporarily soft, and will also be able to develop it when money becomes more available. Moreover, you will not lose whatever equity you have in the property through foreclosure, and will eliminate the payments that were draining your resources.

The investor will get in on the "old" value, generally at a lower interest rate than current purchases, and will not have to put in a down payment. He will also have a knowledgeable partner.

A Scenario

One of my clients bought some very good commercial land on soft terms that allowed for interest-only payments for four years, starting at 4 percent interest and ending at 8 percent. At that point, *amortization*—the paying off of both interest and principal—would begin at a fairly stiff rate. My client planned to have the land developed by that time, and assumed that income from the property would take care of the steeper costs.

My client's plans did not work, and he found himself faced with high payments before the income stream was well developed. In a blaze of genius, he brought in an investor who had a heavy cash flow from his business. My client gave him 49 percent of the equity, and in return, the investor made all monthly payments and covered all expenses until the property was able to support itself. The project was eventually completed, with the last parcel netting the two men more cash than they had originally paid for the entire piece of property.

Using a Syndication to Finance Your Investments

N eed to multiply your investment power for a large-scale project? When your own resources can't supply adequate financing, consider syndication.

As described in the inset on 111, syndication is a method of buying property whereby a syndicator sells shares to other investors. Syndications can take various forms, but all have the same goal—to unite resources for a joint investment that benefits all of the parties involved.

The Strategy

You've found a prime piece of real estate that would be a perfect location for a shopping center. The commercial lender you always deal with, though, will loan you only 75 percent of the purchase price—not nearly enough to finance the project.

Approach the bank for a loan that will be contingent on your finding further financing from other investors. Then have your attorney draw up an agreement for the type of syndication you plan to use.

Now create a private placement offering of the proposed venture that provides the property appraisal; describes the other players in the project, such as the engineering firm; shows the project design; suggests likely anchor stores; details construction costs; supplies a projected cash flow statement; and presents the operating agreement for the syndication being used, as well as the bank's commitment to fund the construction. Present the summary to potential investors, and ask them to participate in the project. (For information on locating partners and coinvestors, see the inset on page 101.)

Once you put together a group that can supply the financing and the operating agreement has been signed, you'll be able to close the deal.

Keep in mind that you must follow your state's guidelines regarding the number of people you can approach and the final number you can admit to the syndication. Generally speaking, if you are soliciting less than $500,000 and bringing in less than thirty-five investors, the process of forming a syndication is relatively simple and quick.

A Scenario

A few years ago, I heard that a friend of mine was in danger of losing the office-warehouse building in which he ran his business. Because his business had seriously deteriorated, he was unable to keep up his payments on the property. The bank that held the loan was therefore ready to foreclose.

The building was well located and of sound construction, and would have been usable for a number of businesses in the area. However, the real estate market had taken a huge hit and had not yet recovered, and if my friend's business failed, the property would likely stay vacant for some time.

I talked to the lender about financing a sale to a group of investors I planned to put together. The building had been sold to my friend for $1,200,000, but because of the depressed market, the lender was asking for $600,000. However, a twin building in the same commercial subdivision had recently sold for $480,000, so the lender agreed to sell the property for $480,000 with a 10-percent down payment, and to charge a lower interest rate on the loan. This would allow us to not only buy the building but also reduce the rent, thus reducing my friend's monthly cash requirements.

An offer was written for $480,000 with $48,000 down, with the lender carrying the balance on a note and first mortgage. After it was accepted, my attorney drew up a limited partnership while I prepared a private placement offering to present to prospective investors. I then solicited eight investors to supply the funding.

Within a week, I had the money needed for the down payment and closing costs, and we closed the deal.

Using a Syndication to Obtain a Loan

In Strategy 30, you saw how syndication can be used to make a real estate purchase. In that scenario, the syndicator was able to secure a conventional loan, and the investors contributed money toward the down payment, with each investor getting an ownership right. Some investments, however—small farms, motels, and cafés, for instance—have little appeal to a lender like a bank, credit union, or insurance company. When you find an investment property such as this, syndication can again be used—this time to borrow small amounts of money from many people to equal the loan you need to finance the purchase. In this case, the investors have no ownership rights, but instead receive interest on the money they loan to the syndication.

The Strategy

A small café has been put up for sale in your town. Situated near the local train station, it is certainly not in a beautiful location, but you think that with a little refurbishing, it will be a real money-maker when early-morning commuters stop by for coffee and rolls. However, you know that no bank will give you the loan you need to buy the property and make the necessary renovations.

To obtain your financing, look for potential investors as outlined in the inset on page 101. Not every investor will be interested in this type of enterprise, but you can honestly point out that the investment makes good sense, because each loan will be secured by a note and first mortgage on the property.

The next step is to break the amount you're looking for into units of a thousand dollars or more. You will structure only one mortgage, but will provide each investor with a separate note for the exact amount he invests.

Once you have commitments for all the units, you'll be able to complete the transaction and buy the café. As you pay the loan off, each investor will get a payment proportional to his interest in the mortgage. Ultimately, each investor will receive his capital back, as well as interest on his portion of the loan.

A Scenario

When the real estate crash of 1979 to 1980 was ending in Alaska, I found a site that would accommodate the construction of ten duplexes. At that time, the conventional lending institutions were not geared for making loans on raw land. Nevertheless, I knew I'd have a winner if I could get the money needed to buy the land and start the construction.

I soon determined that $250,000 would be needed to buy the land, develop the plans, and begin construction on several of the buildings. I then started calling investors to see if they'd be interested in buying portions of a note and mortgage on the property. Each investor was asked for a contribution of $25,000 or more.

After I had secured commitments for $250,000, we closed the loan with several notes totaling $250,000 and a mortgage covering the entire property. Mortgage payments would be made to the investors at six-month intervals, with each investor receiving a portion of his capital plus 12-percent interest.

The development was built, with every unit selling in a single summer, and each investor received his capital and interest back before the last four duplexes were sold.

Understanding Syndication

Strategy 29 explains how you can bring another investor into the picture, and thereby get the financing you need while still retaining a percentage of the equity in your property. But sometimes, as in Strategy 30, one additional investor does not provide enough financing power for the venture you have in mind. True, you can always wait for a smaller deal to come along—one better suited to your resources. But often, a larger, more secure commercial investment makes better sense. In such a case, syndication is often the answer.

Syndication is a method of buying property whereby a sponsor or syndicator—you, in other words—sells interests to other investors. The syndication may take various forms, including that of a limited partnership, a limited liability company, or a corporation. As each of these forms has its own unique structure, benefits, and drawbacks, it pays to briefly examine each in turn.

A *limited partnership* is a form of ownership in which there are two types of partners. Limited partners provide financial backing, but have no role in the management of the property and no personal liability for its debts. But general partners, who are responsible for managing the property, have unlimited personal liability. This means that if someone is a general partner in two or more limited partnerships, and one partnership fails and creates a liability, the general partner's creditors can seek to attach all of his interests in all of his limited partnerships. A limited partnership has pass-through taxation, meaning that the income or loss generated by the syndication passes through to the individual partners for use on their respective income tax returns.

A *limited liability company,* or LLC, is a combination of a corporation and a partnership. The term "limited liability" refers to the fact that like a corporation, the LLC limits personal liability to each of the parties involved, so that members cannot lose more money than they contributed. Personal assets can never be touched. Like limited partnerships, LLCs allow each party to buy units in a property according to the funds he has available. Moreover, members benefit from pass-through taxation.

The corporation is a state-chartered business or organization formed by one or more people, and having rights and liabilities separate from those of the individuals involved. Like the members of an LLC, the members of a corporation are generally not liable for the corporation's debts. Therefore, while the assets of the company may be seized and sold, the assets of the investors cannot be touched. However, the corporation differs from the LLC and limited partnership in that it can sell shares of easily transferable stock. Not all corporations are alike, however. The S corporation has pass-through taxation, but the C corporation is a separate taxable entity, meaning that the profits and losses are taxed directly to the corporation at a corporate income tax rate. Then, distributions made to shareholders are taxed at the rates of the individual shareholders. Because of this double taxation, the returns on any investment may be lower. The earnings of S corporations, limited partnerships, and LLCs are taxed only once.

Clearly, every form of syndication discussed above multiplies your investment power by adding other people's resources to your own. It's worth mentioning that each *also* increases your investment power by allowing both you and other investors to use any money you have in your Individual Retirement Account (IRA). You can even combine discretionary funds (savings) with IRA funds—as long as you follow a few simple rules. If this sounds intriguing, turn to Strategy 43, which focuses on the investment of retirement funds in real estate.

What type of syndication would be best for your particular investment? When choosing a syndication form, keep in mind the benefits you want for both the syndicator and the investors who will participate.

In all forms of syndication, one member—a general partner, a managing member, or a president—is ultimately responsible for obtaining loans and for the actions of the syndication. The corporate form exposes the participants to the least number of risks and responsibilities. When it comes to the loan, however, an individual, rather than the corporate entity, must sign as the responsible party.

Limited liability companies have become popular everywhere because of the limited liability provided for everyone involved, and because of the pass-through taxation—a benefit it shares with S corporations and limited partnerships, of course. Moreover, the LLC, unlike the corporation, does not require yearly shareholders meetings and various other formalities.

Despite the current preference for LLCs, limited partnerships remain an excellent tool for syndication because of the limited liability provided for the investors. But because the general partner *is* exposed to liability, the transaction must offer sufficient benefits to warrant his risks.

When forming a syndication, it's imperative to seek the counsel of a good attorney and an experienced accountant, who will make sure that the transaction is a legal one. Certain properties, for instance, are not eligible for S corporation status. Qualified professionals will provide the guidance you need to select the best form of syndication for your property, and will create an operating agreement that will serve both you and your coinvestors.

Giving Investors a Preferential Interest in Real Estate

There are so many ways to finance a real estate purchase—the number of possibilities is truly staggering! This strategy shows you how to purchase real estate with cash; no borrowed money is used. You can put down a share of the purchase money or, if you prefer, you don't have to put down a dime. Either way, you will earn yearly management fees and even enjoy a profit when the property is eventually sold. Sound too good to be true? It's not!

The Strategy

Interested in finding a building that's selling at a discount, you visit your local bank and ask to talk to their REO (Real Estate Owned) officer, who is in charge of selling foreclosed properties. He tells you about an apartment building that is partially vacant and may need some work. Despite these drawbacks, you feel that the price is great and that the building will appreciate rapidly.

First, make an all-cash offer to the bank, asking for time to secure money from private investors. Once your proposal has been accepted, start calling potential investors and offer them a preferential position in the purchase, meaning that they will get first rights to cash flow, which could well be in excess of current market rates on savings; first rights to getting their investment capital back from either refinancing or sale; and first rights to a large percentage of any profits made from an eventual sale. Since you have found the property, have secured the purchase, and are going to manage it for the group, the investors probably won't mind if you, too, earn some money from the investment.

Now, set up your syndication, and sell interests to your investors. Once the interests have been sold and the financing has been secured, you'll be able to close the deal.

After the closing, be sure to keep in touch with the bank officer. Ask to be advised of any new foreclosures, and have investors ready to spring into action when you call. Good opportunities won't always wait while you arrange financing.

A Scenario

After the Alaska real estate crash of 1986, I found an office building for sale by an out-of-state lender. Only 50-percent occupied, the building was nevertheless reasonably located, and had the potential to be quite profitable.

After crunching the numbers, I determined that I could offer a preferential interest in this property to investors in $25,000 increments, and give them a 10-percent per-year return, with a strong possibility of another 6 percent when the vacancy was filled. Because of the changing real estate market, it seemed likely that the property would double in value during the next five to ten years.

The cost of reconstructing the building and buying the land was about $600,000, and I offered $175,000 in cash. The lender countered with $185,000, and I accepted. I then sold limited partnership interests that totalled $200,000, as I planned to use the excess to refurbish the vacant office space and spruce up the landscaping.

The investors received proportionate interests in the partnership units and a preferential access to the first 10 percent of cash flow. Anything over $20,000 a year—10 percent of $200,000— would be divided, with 60 percent going to them, and 40 percent going to me. Any future refinancing or sale that produced cash would first be used to pay back the partners' original investment, with any balance again being split 60-40. I also was to receive a fee for managing the assets of the limited partnership.

Deal-Making Strategy
Using a Life Insurance Annuity to Obtain the Property You Want

S trategy 18 showed that not all potential property sellers are looking for a buyer who offers the standard lump sum of cash. Some would prefer to exchange their real estate for worry-free housing. Still others, however, are looking for something else—a steady income that would allow them to live comfortably for the rest of their lives. That's where the life insurance annuity comes in.

Life insurance annuity policies provide a set monthly cash payment to the beneficiary, based on his age and the amount of money paid for the policy. In some cases—most often when the property owner is older—the purchase of an annuity will not only allow you to make the deal, but will allow you to make the deal more profitable. If the seller is looking for a steady income in return for his property, this strategy can enable you to buy the property for an amount *below* fair market value, while providing the seller with a lifetime income that he might not have been able to secure by investing the proceeds of a cash sale.

The Strategy

Let's say that you have found a piece of property which you feel would be a great investment. However, you are reluctant to pay the asking price of the owner—an elderly man who plans to use the proceeds of the sale to finance his retirement, and therefore is demanding an above-market amount.

First, determine exactly what the seller wants in terms of monthly income. Then contact a life insurance company, and find out how much you would have to pay to buy an annuity in the seller's name that would make regular payments in that amount. Of course, the person's age, the type of the annuity purchased, and even the state of the economy will have an effect on the amount of money needed, but an insurance agent will be able to give you current figures. The goal, of course, is to purchase the property at below market value by using all cash, and at the same time give the seller exactly what he wants in terms of income.

The Scenario

An elderly carpet layer listed his property with a broker at $180,000, a price $20,000 above fair market value. No offers were forthcoming, and when the listing expired, he decided to take the property off the market, claiming that capital gains taxes would eat up his profits. In reality, he had discovered that the net cash he would receive from the sale would not give him the income he was looking for—$1,000 a month.

A local corporation needed the carpet layer's land, but balked at paying more than it was worth to get it. When the corporation became aware of the owner's true goal of getting a regular monthly income, the solution became apparent. After doing some research, they realized that they could buy the carpet layer the income he wanted by investing only $144,183 in an annuity—an amount lower than both the asking price and the market value.

The corporation's offer was accepted, and the deal was closed. The seller knew that once the annuity had been purchased, and for the rest of his life, the check would arrive each month like clockwork. He smiled all the way to southern California.

Raising the Interest
and Lowering the Price

Common sense tells you that it's better to pay low interest than high interest on a mortgage. If the price of the property remains the same but the rate of interest is increased, the amount of money paid over time can go up quite a bit. That's why many an investor understands the wisdom of the statement, "You name the price and I'll name the terms."

But what if the interest goes up and the price goes down, rather than remaining the same? If calculated correctly, this strategy allows a buyer who's low on immediate cash to afford the property he wants, and to ultimately pay the same amount he would have paid if he had agreed to the original terms, or—because interest is tax-deductible—to pay even *less*.

The Strategy

You have found an income property that would make a fine addition to your real estate portfolio. However, at the moment you have little ready cash for the down payment.

Before approaching the buyer, make some calculations to determine how you can lower the asking price but raise the rate of interest so that your down payment is lower, yet ultimately, you will pay the same amount for the house that the seller is demanding. Remember that with higher interest payments, you will be getting back more money every year at tax time. After the write-off, you may even end up paying less!

Once your computations are complete, approach the seller and offer the new terms. Point out that if he finances the sale by carrying back the note, he will get the same number of dollars in the long run. And if he ever decides to sell the note, the high interest rate will make it salable at a higher price.

A Scenario

A client of mine wanted income-producing property in a specific area, and I soon found an apartment house for sale in the desired location. The owner and his wife, both retired, had managed the property for many years, and now wanted to be free to travel and enjoy other leisure activities. The only problem was that the owner was asking $300,000, while the market indicated a value of about $260,000.

My client understandably balked at paying the inflated price. Moreover, his financial situation limited the money he could put on the table as a down payment. However, I knew that although his ready cash was in short supply, he enjoyed good cash flow from other investments; monthly payments would be no problem for him. I therefore suggested that he offer the market price for the property, but at the same time propose an interest rate higher than the owner had suggested. A simple chart showed him how the two scenarios would affect the final cost of the apartment house:

PRICE	INTEREST RATE	MONTHLY PAYMENT	TERM OF LOAN
$300,000	10 percent	$2, 895	20 Years
$260,000	12.18 percent	$2, 895	20 Years

My client requested a clause that would allow him to pay off the balance at any time he wished. The seller, of course, immediately recognized that if the loan was paid off quickly, he would lose money. The two men therefore agreed that the loan could not be paid off within the first ten years, and that if the loan was paid off during the last ten years, there would be a penalty, which would decrease with time.

The sale benefited everyone involved. My client paid what he felt was a fair price, made a reasonable down payment, and enjoyed tax deductions as a result of the higher interest rate. And, of course, he got the property he wanted and needed for his portfolio. The seller, on the other hand, received close to his asking price, and knew he would receive the exact number of dollars he wanted if the loan was allowed to continue for the full twenty years. Best of all, he had a buyer who was financially capable of handling all payments.

Raising the Price
and Lowering the Interest

I n Strategy 34, you learned how you can help finance a purchase by lowering the price and increasing the interest rate—a strategy that, if used properly, will allow you to put less money down on the sale, while giving the seller the final amount of cash that he wants.

Strategy 35 focuses on the exact reverse of that one—raising the price and decreasing the interest rate. Why would you want to do that? If you've ever been unable to borrow the money you needed because the property that secured the loan was not of sufficient value, this technique will make immediate sense to you. By establishing a higher-priced asset, this strategy will help you get a larger loan.

The Strategy

You have found an investment property that has great potential. However, the property has been vacant for some time, and needs to be renovated to attract a new tenant. The asking price is below the assessed value. In order to get the loan that you need, you have to establish a higher sales price. But, understandably, you are reluctant to pay both a high price and the market interest rate.

Offer a higher-than-listed sales price but a below-market interest rate. Then promise to secure a maximum conventional loan and to give most of the money to the seller, who will carry back a note and a second mortgage on top of the bank loan. When the conventional lender sees the high purchase price and the appraisal, he shouldn't hesitate to give you the loan you want.

A Scenario

One of my friends owned a property valued at $120,000. A $70,000 balloon payment was due on his mortgage, and he had been unable to raise the money to pay off the debt. Due to the property's mostly unimproved state, none of the lenders in the area were willing to make a loan on it.

My friend knew that he needed to find another property to serve as security for his loan. He soon located one that had been on the market for a year, and was free and clear. The owner, a widow, was running a small business in a building that she and her husband had built eight years before. The business was not doing well, but she had enough money to retire comfortably without it. The property had been appraised and assessed by the county at $109,000, but due to overbuilding, lack of use, and the fact that it had been on the market for a year without any offers, the owner had lowered the price to $75,000.

In exchange for her property, my friend offered the seller a created note and mortgage on his vacant land in the amount of $75,000. What my friend didn't realize was that banks generally will loan 75 percent of the sales price or the appraisal, whichever is *less*. The bank, therefore, would lend him only about $56,000— 75 percent of the sales price of $75,000.

My friend took out his calculator and began to think creatively. His first offer had been $75,000 at 12 percent interest. That would mean payments of $826 per month. If he offered $95,000 at 9 percent interest, the payments would be $856 a month for the same period, or only $30 more a month. If the bank would accept the $95,000 purchase price—which seemed likely, as the property had been assessed at $109,000—it should be willing to make a loan of about $71,000, which was slightly more than my friend needed to make his balloon payment.

My friend resubmitted the loan application showing the increased price, and the bank came through with a loan of $71,250. The bank did not care about the interest rate—only the purchase price and payment terms.

Since the seller was looking for additional cash, she and my friend made a bargain. If my friend decided to pay the entire mortgage off within the first year, he could do so for $75,000, a 21-percent discount. To give him further motivation to pay off the created note and mortgage in the early years, she reduced the discount each year so that if he decided to pay it off during the second year, he could pay the existing balance due minus $9,000; during the third year, the balance less $8,000; and so on, through the first ten years. It was to my friend's benefit to pay off his debt as soon as possible.

Performing Due Diligence

The scenarios presented throughout this book involve the purchase of properties ranging from single-family homes to motels to apartment buildings, and even vacant lots. Because this book focuses on the financing of these transactions, rather than the process used to select them, none of the scenarios covers the topic of due diligence. But anyone who wants to make smart real estate investments should understand the importance of due diligence, and know how to perform it prior to making a purchase.

Due diligence is a careful study performed of the physical, financial, legal, and social characteristics of a specific piece of property, and of its predicted investment performance. This study is a vital part of *any* real estate purchase, because it can tell you whether the investment you're considering will increase your financial strength or drain it away. Some of the questions that due diligence should answer are:

❑ What is the physical condition of the building, including the roof, windows, foundation, and electrical systems? Will repairs be needed, and if so, at what cost?

❑ How does the asking price compare with the appraised value of the property?

❑ Will you be able to get clear title to the property, or are there liens or attachments on it?

❑ If the building is an apartment house or other income-producing property, what is its *cash flow*—the net income that will be available from its rental after all necessary expenditures? In other words: What is the tax bill? What is the utility bill? What is the insurance bill? And after paying all these bills, how much income will remain?

❑ What changes, if any, appear to be taking place in that area? For instance, are development and industry moving toward your property? Has a new highway been planned? If so, your property may rise in value.

❏ What are the supply-and-demand conditions in that area for that specific type of property? If it's an office building, for example, is there presently a demand for office space, or is there a glut of office space?

How can you answer these questions? If possible, begin by visiting the property under consideration. Nothing can compare with an on-site examination—not just of the property itself, but also of the area around it. Are other buildings in the area being renovated and improved, or are they being allowed to deteriorate? Are upscale stores opening in the vicinity, or are many businesses steering clear of the area? Even a casual visit can often provide important answers.

If the property includes a building, you'll want to seek expert advice on its physical condition. Is the roof sound? Is the electrical system up to code? A qualified property inspector can give you detailed information about the structure and the systems within it, allowing you to make an informed decision about your investment.

Naturally, you'll want to determine if the asking price makes sense. If no appraisal is available on the real estate in question, have your broker research comparable properties in that area. An experienced realtor should have no problem finding current sales figures for several similar properties. A careful examination of these figures may even show whether prices in the area are in the process of rising or falling.

Is the title to the property clear of lien? Are there any defects that could restrict you from taking full ownership? A title search will provide you with this important information. In some states, your attorney is responsible for having a title search completed, while in other states, the buyer works directly with the title company, which searches the property's chain of title. If you don't already know how title searches are handled in your area, a local realtor will be able to fill you in.

If you're buying an apartment building, an office building, a motel, or any other income-producing property, you'll want to perform careful financial research, which means that you'll want to look at tax returns, income and expense statements, property tax statements, and leases. Keep in mind that statements of both income and expenses are often intentionally misleading. Unless you have considerable experience in this area and are well qualified to analyze these statements and detect any inconsistencies, have a qualified accountant crunch the numbers and give you a realistic appraisal of the property's current performance.

Finally, when appropriate, don't hesitate to spend some time observing the operation of any small real estate business venture, such as a motel, bakery, or dry cleaning establishment. If, for instance, the current owner states that on the average weekend, the business pulls in such-and-such an amount of revenue, spend a weekend there working beside the owner or manager. If you are knowledgeable about that type of business, you should be able to judge whether the owner's figures are valid.

There's no doubt that due diligence involves hard work. Its value, however, cannot be overemphasized. Good due diligence can mean the difference between a purchase that builds your real estate portfolio, and one that drains cash away by failing to perform as expected. Even if you have to call in an accountant or other professional to aid in research and analysis, the money you spend on due diligence will be nominal compared with what you have to gain—and what you stand to lose.

Using a Performance Purchase Price

Many sellers of income properties fail to provide potential buyers with accurate information regarding their property's performance. It's quite common for owners to report expenses to the hilt, but, as a means of keeping taxes low, to declare only a portion of their income. This is especially true of taverns, motels, grocery stores, resorts, and other real estate business ventures that allow the operator to hide income.

Don't you wish that you could base the sales price on the property's actual performance, and therefore pay only what it's worth, as opposed to what the owner says it's worth? Well, you can—by using the performance purchase price.

The Strategy

You have found a motel for sale. While you feel that the business will be a good income producer, based on the figures provided by the owner, you can't see paying the asking price.

Structure the sale or exchange with an undetermined price, allowing the price to be based on the future performance of the property under your management. Agree that the final price will be equal to four times the average of the first two years' gross income. In the meantime, each month, you will pay 20 percent of the business's gross income on the carryback paper the seller holds.

When two years are up, you and the seller will do the math, arrive at the sales price, and determine what your remaining monthly payments will be. And you'll know that you're paying what the property and business are worth.

A Scenario

A client was interested in buying a tavern. Having been injured in an industrial accident, and therefore limited in the work he could do, he planned to have his son-in-law run the tavern, which, he hoped, would provide him with the money he needed to retire.

The tavern he liked was a little spotty on records, and the seller had the typical story about the large number of kegs he sold, his carryout business, the pool table income, the vending machine income, and more. Some of it we could confirm, and some we couldn't. At any rate, it soon became apparent that to protect himself, my client would have to base his payments on the tavern's actual income. He therefore structured an agreement with the following conditions:

1. Each month, he would pay 20 percent of the tavern's gross income towards the contract.

2. At the end of two years, the total amount paid to the owner would be divided by twenty-four months, and the average amount would, from that time on, be the permanent monthly payment.

3. The permanent monthly payment would represent some total mortgage amount, amortized over fifteen years at 8-percent interest.

During the first two years, my client paid $58,944, which, when divided by 24, equaled $2,456 average monthly payment. My client and the seller determined that this payment made over fifteen years at 8 percent interest would amortize a loan of $256,997. In this way, they agreed on the amount yet to be paid on the tavern—an amount that would be fair to both the buyer and the seller.

Motivating a Lender With a Loan-to-Equity Option

In various strategies throughout this book, we've discussed ways to motivate hesitant lenders to give you the financing you need. Once you start thinking creatively, so many possibilities present themselves! Here's one that works well when arranging loans on income-producing properties. Insert a clause in the loan agreement that will give the lender the option to convert the loan to equity. This will provide the lender with an opportunity to increase his yield—and to become a participant *after* the property is producing income and the degree of risk is much lower. And, of course, it will give you the cash you need to pursue your venture.

The Strategy

Let's say that you own a parcel of land free and clear, and you need money to build a shopping center. Approach a lender who can legally own property—an insurance company, union fund, or private lender—and request a loan, offering to insert a conversion-to-equity clause in the loan agreement.

If the lender agrees, you'll have your loan. But be careful. Problems can occur if the lender exercises the option but does not have the knowledge to make wise business decisions, owns too much of the project, or is controlled by a board of directors that doesn't have a personal relationship with you, the borrower. To avoid these difficulties, you'll want to include clauses that will protect you from any heavy-handed treatment. For instance:

1. If the lender decides to convert the loan to equity, he will become a limited partner only.

2. Conversion of the loan to equity can take place only after giving ample notice to the borrower.

3. The lender must join in signing any new loans—or agree to sell or exchange when the borrower decides to sell or exchange.

When drafting the agreement, always keep in mind that the loan is a two-way street, and that the lender and borrower must both get reasonable benefits from the arrangement.

A Scenario

A local builder had the opportunity to buy land zoned for apartments at a very low price due to the motivation of the seller and the fact that the property did not yet have sewer service. The builder contacted local lenders, and found none willing to make a loan on the undeveloped land. He then contacted a realtor who guided him to an employees' pension trust fund.

The pension fund agreed to loan the builder the money with the provision that in the future, it could convert the loan to equity and become a limited partner at a price determined by an appraiser of the lender's choosing. If the owner didn't like the appraisal, he could order a second appraisal. If the builder and the lender still could not reach an agreement, the two appraisers were to hire a third appraiser.

Due to a zoning cutback and a master plan drawn up by the community, the land increased in value rapidly, moving from $160,000 to $240,000 during the year after the land's purchase. Wisely, the lender converted his loan to equity. As it turned out, though, neither party hired an appraiser. Instead, they used the new assessed valuation as fair market value.

Motivating a Lender With a Loan-to-Stock Option

S trategy 37 showed you how to motivate a hesitant lender by giving him an option to convert the loan to equity in the property at some future time. If you are seeking financing for a corporation rather than an individual, yet another possibility is available—offering the lender an option to convert the loan to stocks.

In a situation such as this, the lender's hope, of course, is to exchange the loan for stock when the stock is rising in value, and then sell it at the top of the market. Thus, the lender stands to make far more money than he would if the loan was simply paid off at current interest rates.

The Strategy

Let's say that you are the president of a small corporation, and you need money to buy the vacant lot next to your office building and construct a new warehouse that will better meet the needs of your growing business.

Because you own a small company—one of three to ten people—you'll have the best chance of getting your loan if you approach a private lender. Request the loan, offering to insert a conversion-to-stocks clause in the agreement. If the lender agrees, make sure that the loan document contains clauses that will protect you and your company. For instance:

1. The lender must wait a specific period of time—usually, three to ten years—before converting the loan to stock.

2. When the conversion takes place, every dollar of the loan balance will be converted into shares of stock, either at a previously agreed-upon price or at the current market value.

3. The treasury of the corporation must have an adequate amount of stock left—and may be required to maintain the stock on hand during the life of the loan.

4. The lender is not allowed to put all of its stock on the market at once during certain market conditions. Moreover, the corporation has the right of first refusal to repurchase its stock should the lender decide to sell.

As mentioned earlier, if your corporation is a small one, you'll want to approach a small lender. If, however, you have a large corporation whose stock is on the market and has cash market value, you can work with any lender.

A Scenario

A local corporation was formed to pick up old mining claims. The risk was high, but the potential profit was enormous.

The corporation needed cash to buy gold mining equipment. If the price of gold kept rising and the mines yielded the expected amount of gold, the company's stockholders stood to make big money. First, however, they needed $60,000 to purchase the necessary tools.

Another local corporation loaned the mining company the money, with the agreement that the loan could be converted to stock at the option of the lender. Since the principals in the mining corporation knew one another as well as the lender, there was a daily exchange of information over coffee. Right after the mining company agreed to merge with a multinational corporation at a considerable increase in the value of the company's stock, the lender converted the loan to stock shares—just prior to the due date of the first loan payment. After the merger, the lender sold its shares and recovered $87,500 on its $60,000 loan. Because the lender was selling the stock of the larger multinational corporation, rather than the small company to which it had made the loan, all of the shares could be sold at once without creating a problem.

Splitting Up
the Down Payment

Most sellers ask for a large down payment, and most buyers offer a small down payment. Most sellers want the balance to be paid in a short period of time, while most buyers want to make smaller payments over a longer period of time. Everyone is used to this "dance," and anticipates it. That's why, as a buyer, you will have a psychological advantage if you make an offer that differs from the usual. One way to achieve this is to offer to split up the down payment—to pay it out over a period of years. You can then treat the balance as a separate entity to be paid only after the full down payment has been received.

The Strategy

You have found the perfect income-producing property. It's in a good location, and it has excellent growth potential. The only problem is that the owner wants a huge down payment.

Offer a portion of the down payment at closing, a portion in the next tax year, and a portion in the third tax year. This will scatter the down payment over three tax years, and allow the property itself to help make the payments. You can offer interest on the unpaid principal, often at a lesser rate than the underlying mortgage.

If you wish, and if the seller agrees, make future installments of the down payment subject to certain specified conditions—

reaching projected rent or occupancy rates or a break-even cash flow, for instance.

Then deal separately with the principal balance left after the full down payment has been made, offering a payment schedule, interest rate, and any balloon payment suitable to the market on that portion alone. The seller will adjust psychologically and often move with you on these points. He will come to understand that the down payment and the balance are two different entities.

A Scenario

Years ago, I listed a fifty-unit apartment house for $2,300,000. The owner asked for $500,000 down, with the balance being paid over twenty-five years at 11 percent interest. He still owed about $1,400,000 at 10.25 percent interest, payable over twenty-four years.

A prospective purchaser was found by another agent who offered the full asking price, but split the down payment into three portions: $200,000 at closing, which was to be in December; $150,000 to be paid eight months later, in the next tax year; and the remaining $150,000 to be paid twelve months after the second payment. Interest on the remaining unpaid down payment was 10 percent.

After the final installment of the down payment, interest-only payments on the balance of $1,800,000 were to be made at 11-percent. In eight years, a balloon payment of the remaining principal would completely repay the loan. The property was also to be leased back by the seller for one year to prove that his stated operating income and expenses were accurate.

The purchaser benefited by acquiring a prime property for an initial down payment of only about 9 percent of the total purchase price. He was also able to spread the down payment out over three years, making it easier to come up with the remaining cash. And he received tremendous tax benefits during those three years because of the leverage produced by the initial small down payment and the succeeding interest-only payments.

The seller could look forward to having large increments of cash infused into his personal finances over the next three years. Moreover, because of the arrangement, he had a stronger buyer.

Splitting the Profits

This twist on owner financing can sometimes be used to purchase new construction—whether a private residence or a commercial building—that is being bought from the builder. The purchaser makes a conventional down payment, but buys the property at below market value, at a price that equals only the builder's costs and overhead. In exchange for selling the house at this discounted price, the builder retains a portion of the profits from future sales.

The Strategy

You have found your dream house in a new development. The price, however, is somewhat beyond your means at this time. In fact, you notice that no one's snapping up these houses very quickly.

Offer to buy the house at below market value—at a price that will equal the builder's costs and overhead and pay off his construction loan, but will provide no profits. You might start by offering approximately 75 to 80 percent of the asking price. Further suggest that the builder retain a 50-percent interest in future profits from any resale. He will then be able to enjoy additional income in years to come—income that may be enhanced by appreciation. You, of course, will be acquiring your house at a bargain price, and will receive full benefits of tax write-offs and principal reduction on the loan.

Will every builder jump at this arrangement? Obviously not. But in some situations, the builder will be happy to pay off his debt so that he can move on to other projects. And he'll know that a payoff is coming to him down the road.

A Scenario

A local builder had two unsold houses remaining in his subdivision. All the other homes had been sold, and the builder had begun work on another subdivision in another part of town. These two homes, however, were not moving, but were simply eating up money as the builder made monthly payments to the lender.

A client—an investor—asked me to negotiate an offer on the two homes. He suggested that we make a cash offer at 75 percent of the asking price. I presented the offer to the builder, who laughed but said he'd think about it.

The next day, the builder called and said that he would accept the offer, provided that he could retain 50-percent ownership in future profits. My client agreed, and the transaction was closed.

After various improvements such as landscaping had been made, the houses appreciated in value, with both homes selling for far more than the original asking price. Eventually, my client and the builder each received $40,000 from the sale of the two buildings.

Using
Balloon Payments

S ometimes, a lack of capital and cash flow makes it impossible to purchase a piece of property on the seller's terms. Yet you know that because of a future event, such as the upcoming sale of a sizable asset, you will have the capital you need within a year or two. In such a case, you may be able to arrange the purchase by offering a small initial down payment and lower monthly payments, with several balloon payments—keyed to the dates at which the money will be available—that will eventually satisfy the loan in full.

The Strategy

Your realtor has told you about an office building that has just been put up for sale. In great condition and situated in a prime location, this property promises to be a valuable addition to your portfolio. At the moment, you don't have sufficient money for a standard down payment. But you know that in a year, some of your frozen assets will become liquid, and you'll have the cash.

Determine the kind of down payment you are able to make, as well as when your circumstances will allow you to provide one or more balloon payments to pay off the loan. Then make your offer to the seller, providing specific dates so that he'll know exactly when he will get his money. If possible, present evidence that the cash will indeed be available at that time. He'll want to know that your promises are based on actual future events, rather than wishful thinking.

When you and the seller have agreed on terms that are acceptable to both of you, you'll be able to close the deal.

A Scenario

A client of mine was interested in buying an apartment house that was up for sale near his place of business. The structure was in very good condition, and all of the units had tenants. My client knew that the property would be a great income producer. The only problem was that the seller was asking for $300,000, with a 30-percent down payment. As interested as my client was, he simply could not afford to put down $90,000.

My client mulled over the problem, and when he noticed that no other buyer was offering the down payment demanded by the seller, he had an idea. My client knew that in two years, he would be finished closing out his father's estate and would be made a partner in his law firm, thus allowing him a percentage of the firm's profits. He therefore offered to make a 10-percent down payment of $30,000, with another 5 percent down in two years; 5 percent, the year after that; and 10 percent, the year after that.

After some hesitation, the seller accepted the offer, and my client acquired a property that is still producing a constant stream of income for him.

Deal-Making Strategy
Removing a Second
Mortgage to Make a Deal

I n Strategy 2, you learned about the option of trading one piece of real estate for another in lieu of paying cash for your purchase. While this type of transaction is made all the time, clearly, the road to these trades is not always a smooth one. Sometimes, for instance, owners are not comfortable trading their property for real estate that has a second mortgage on it. They simply feel that the second mortgage makes the deal too risky. The solution? Often, the holder of the second mortgage can be persuaded to remove it from your old property and place it as a first mortgage on the new property. Once the second mortgage has been removed, the deal can go through.

The Strategy

Let's say that you own a commercial building and wish to trade it for some raw land, which you'll use to build a shopping center in an area that's undergoing growth and development. The commercial building is in good condition, with a low-interest first mortgage and a small higher-interest second mortgage. Unfortunately, the owner of the raw land is a very cautious man who does not believe in second mortgages.

Approach the holder of the second mortgage, and ask him to remove it and place it on the land as a first mortgage. If he seems hesitant to do so, make the arrangement more attractive by raising the interest rate a little or speeding up the payoff. Clearly, in this instance, you are the one who is motivated to shift the mortgage, so you may have to extend yourself a bit and make the terms more favorable for the lender.

Another option is to ask the holder of the second mortgage to move the loan to the other property as a second, provided that he approves of the property. Again, you may have to extend yourself by improving the terms, as you are the one who will benefit from the change.

A Scenario

A large firm owned numerous commercial properties in and around a city. During a time of recession, several of the company's office buildings became 100-percent vacant. In order to retain ownership of the buildings during the two-year lull, the firm placed small second mortgages on them above the old first mortgages. This gave the firm the cash it needed to satisfy the first mortgages and to pay expenses.

When the economy started growing again, the company desperately needed some additional warehouse space, and sought a site for the new building. The firm found the perfect piece of property and offered to exchange one of their buildings for the land. The only problem was that the land was owned by a crusty old railroad worker who wanted and needed cash flow, but would not accept a property that had a second mortgage on it.

The firm contacted the private party who held the second mortgage, and by offering a fee of 1-percent of the loan, persuaded him to remove the mortgage from the building and place it on the land as a first mortgage. The deal then went through to everyone's advantage. The railroad worker enjoyed a steady stream of income from his new building. The firm acquired the land it needed for a warehouse. And the holder of the second mortgage made a bit more than he would have if the mortgage had remained on the building—plus, he was now in first position on the land.

Using Self-Directed IRA Funds to Finance a Real Estate Purchase

What's the best-kept secret in the world of real estate? *It's perfectly legal to use funds from your Individual Retirement Account (IRA) to purchase real estate.* That's right. Contrary to what most people believe, you don't have to limit the investment of your retirement funds to stocks and CDs. Instead, you can use the money in your IRA to buy a retirement home, an apartment building, an office complex—whatever property you have in mind. And as long as you follow the rules set down by the government (see the inset on page 148), not only will your investment be legal, but—depending on whether you have a traditional IRA or a Roth—your profits will be either tax-deferred or tax-free!

The Strategy

A parking lot near your place of work just went up for sale. Located in an area that's become a magnet for new businesses, the lot promises to be a real moneymaker. The only problem is that you don't have the ready cash needed for a down payment. On the other hand, you *do* have a fair amount of money in your IRA, and it's earning almost nothing in a money market account.

The first step in making your retirement funds available for real estate investments is to convert your traditional or Roth IRA into a self-directed IRA. This account can be established with any one of the two dozen or so administrators out there. (See the list of Selected IRA Trustees and Custodians on page 187.) It is a simple matter of filling out a one-page application and sending in a small check. Your funds will then be transferred from your existing IRA to a new self-directed account that will allow you to invest your retirement savings as you wish.

Then proceed with the purchase just as you would if you were buying the property with regular savings. As usual, either your attorney or your real estate broker will draw up the necessary documents, such as the contract of sale. In this case, however, the paperwork will ultimately be sent to your IRA administrator, who will approve the deal and provide the funding—typically, by making a wire transfer directly from your retirement account to the escrow company.

Note that the property will be purchased in the name of your IRA, and not in your name. Similarly, all income from the property—and, ultimately, from the sale of the property—will go directly into your Individual Retirement Account.

A Scenario

One of my clients was tired of the ups and downs of the stock market, and had decided to invest funds from his Roth IRA in income-producing property. He had $400,000 in his retirement account, and wished to avoid all debt. The existing funds had to be sufficient for the investment.

After examining several properties, I found a local fast-food restaurant for sale. The tenant was three years into a ten-year lease, and had two five-year options to extend. Moreover, the tenant had a *triple-net lease,* meaning that he would pay all of the property's operating costs, including utilities, taxes, and insurance. After expenses, the cash flow was $30,000 annually. The asking price was $350,000.

My client was interested, so I made an offer. Because I was working with a ready supply of cash, the deal was not subject to financing and could close quickly. I therefore was able to offer $325,000—$25,000 less than the asking price—and we quickly made a deal. Once the papers were drawn up, they were sent to my client's IRA administrator for approval. Because his IRA administrator does not allow account holders to manage IRA-owned property, my client had to hire a professional property management company to collect the rent and pay the bills. But even after covering the management company's fees, his IRA was soon receiving $2,300 a month.

What IRA Transactions Are Prohibited?

Although your IRA provides cash for a host of investments, it's important to understand that the government has set up IRAs so that they hold retirement funds in trust for you. This money, then, is not regarded as *your* money, and certain types of transactions are prohibited. These transactions include the following:

❑ Your IRA cannot do business with any disqualified person, including your husband or wife, your natural parents, your natural grandparents, your natural children and their spouses, your adoptive parents, your adopted children, or anyone involved in the administration of your IRA. The list of disqualified people, by the way, also includes *you*.

❑ You cannot use funds from your IRA in an investment whose primary purpose is to benefit you or another party, rather than your IRA. In other words, the primary purpose of any IRA investments must be the enhancement of your Individual Retirement Account.

❑ You cannot borrow money from your IRA, nor can you borrow money against an asset that is owned by your IRA.

❑ You cannot use your IRA funds to make a loan to a corporation or partnership when 50 percent or more of the stock or unit ownership in that company is held by you or by another disqualified person.

❑ You cannot purchase life insurance with your IRA.

❑ You cannot use your IRA to invest in any property considered to be a collectible by the IRS. This property includes, but is not limited to, works of art, rugs, antiques, metals, gems, stamps, coins, and alcoholic beverages.

Despite these restrictions, many great investment opportunities remain. Nevertheless, when using your IRA to finance real estate, it's vital to work with both an attorney and an accountant who are familiar with the rules that govern IRA transactions, and can help insure that your investments stay well within the boundaries of the law.

Getting Cash Out
of a Second Mortgage

As a real estate investor, you may, at some point, sell some of your property as a means of financing other projects. This is an effective financing strategy—as long as the person who buys your property is able to make a down payment sufficiently large to meet your needs. A problem occurs, though, when the sale results in a smaller-than-desired down payment and a large second mortgage. How can such a transaction yield the immediate money you want and still provide you with the long-term benefits of cash flow from the note? If you are carrying back a note on the second mortgage, the following strategy can give you a blast of cash, as well as some cash flow.

The Strategy

Let's say that you want cash for a new real estate venture, and to get it, you decide to sell a commercial building that you have owned for many years. You finally find a buyer, and are eager to make the deal. The plan is that he will assume your first mortgage, and you will carry back a note and second mortgage. While, of course, the second mortgage will provide you with a dependable stream of cash over the coming years, your reason for selling the property is to get an *immediate* sum that will allow you to launch your new venture. Unfortunately, the buyer can't make a down payment that is sufficiently large to meet your investment needs.

Instead of carrying back a large second mortgage, create a small second mortgage—one that you can sell on the discount market to provide an immediate infusion of cash. Then carry back a note and third mortgage to cover the remaining equity.

Are there risks involved in carrying back a third mortgage note? Absolutely. If the buyer fails to make his mortgage payments, and the property is foreclosed and sold to pay his debts, you will be third in line to receive any money, with the holders of the first and second mortgages receiving the first proceeds of the sale. However, you will at least have enjoyed the benefits of the cash, and will be in no worse shape than you would have been had you foreclosed on a second mortgage.

A Scenario

A local investor first built a fortune in raw land, and then started developing his properties. He found himself in trouble with his bank, though, when it demanded that he immediately pay $100,000 on some of his notes. He then began cruising the real estate market, trying to sell one of his subdivisions.

I made an offer that supplied the investor with $75,000 of the necessary cash. Now all he needed was another $25,000. Since he was carrying back a substantial second mortgage on the transaction, the payments from which he would have to pledge to the bank anyway, I suggested that he create a smaller second for $35,000, sell the second at a discount, and carry back the remainder of his equity on a note and third mortgage.

Although the investor disliked selling paper at a discount, he agreed. The $35,000 note was sold for $25,000 cash, and the remaining $150,000 equity was carried as a third mortgage. And the investor got the bank off his back.

Filling the Gap
With a Bridge Loan

You have a compelling reason to purchase a piece of real estate, and time is running out to get the financing you need from a conventional lender. The transaction is in escrow, the legal documents are drawn, and everyone expects the loan to come through today or tomorrow—but it doesn't. You can, of course, take this as a sign that the investment wasn't meant to be. Or you can apply for a bridge loan.

Also known as a swing loan, a *bridge loan* is a short-term loan for borrowers who need time to secure permanent financing. The bridge loan, which can be arranged within just a few days, permits you to act quickly and take advantage of real estate opportunities as they present themselves.

The Strategy

An apartment house just went up for sale in your area. It's in a great location, and couldn't be in better condition. Your plan is to form a limited liability company with a group of other investors and purchase the apartment building together. The only problem is that this will take time, and you're afraid that someone will snap up the property before you can get the funding you need.

Approach a bank or another lender, and apply for a bridge loan. Banks and other primary lenders, such as investment trust companies and credit unions, have short-term deposits on hand, and are always looking for ways to put that money to use for short, defined periods of time. Generally, a commercial lending officer in the bank's loan department will assess your application and present it to the loan committee.

As the name implies, a bridge loan is designed to bridge the gap between a purchase and the acquisition of permanent financing. Many people use the bridge loan to make a down payment on a new house while arranging the sale of an old house, and waiting for the resulting profits. But bridge loans can also be used to fund construction of a new building, to renovate an older property, or to keep a rental afloat until rents are raised and cash flow improves.

Just be aware that while bridge loans can be lifesavers, they come at a high cost. Interest rates are high, points are high, and costs and fees are involved. Often the cost of a bridge loan is equal to that of a permanent loan—some 3 to 5 percent of the loan amount. So before you apply for the loan, make sure that no other form of immediate financing is available to you.

A Scenario

I had put together a five-property exchange with a past client, who had $2.5 million in equity coming from a 1031 Starker exchange. (To learn about Starker exchanges, see page 27.) In order to meet the terms of the exchange agreement and close the transaction, we needed a $5 million loan with some stringent terms and conditions specified by my client.

The loan broker with whom we were working assured us that he could nail down the required loan in time for the closing. So we went about supplying him with the figures and papers he needed to complete the loan.

When the time of the closing arrived, the loan didn't. I negotiated a short extension of the exchange agreement, and we started looking for another lender. The loan broker came up with a local bank that would provide a $5 million two-year bridge loan at reasonable interest rates, with a promise to consider extending it for another year if necessary. After persuading the bank to extend the term of the loan to three years, we closed the deal.

Once the deal was closed, the team managing my client's new income property began to raise the rents to market levels. By the time the loan came due, cash flow had improved and it was relatively easy to secure permanent financing.

Securing a Low-Interest Loan at Foreclosure

When the owner of real estate fails to make payments on his mortgage, the bank—or whatever other institution or person holds the mortgage—goes through the foreclosure process, in which the owner is deprived of the right to redeem the mortgaged property. Moreover, some cities and counties actively foreclose on properties that are abandoned, delinquent in taxes, or causing a public menace. Whatever the reason for the foreclosure, it is followed by a foreclosure sale, which is the public sale of the property. Proceeds of the sale are used to repay the debt.

Foreclosure sales have always been an opportunity waiting to happen. Because the holder of the mortgage is eager to receive the money owed to him, he is usually willing to accept a price that is far below the property's market value. Occasionally, municipalities—whose chief motive is to get the property back on the tax rolls—will even accept very small down payments. But perhaps most important, the mortgage holder is often willing to accept a below-market interest rate, if only for the relatively short time it takes you to renovate the house in preparation for rental or sale.

The Strategy

Let's say that you are in the market for a good rental house. Since your funds are limited, you decide to look at foreclosures.

There are a number of different ways to discover which properties are being foreclosed in your area. As a first step, try checking the foreclosure section in your local newspaper. Lists of foreclosures are also often made available on the Internet. Finally, visit your local bank and introduce yourself to the REO (Real Estate Owned) officer, who is in charge of selling foreclosed properties. Once you become acquainted with the officer, you might request that he keep you informed of any interesting properties that become available.

When you find real estate that you feel has potential, consider the type of problems you will face while getting the property back on the market. How much money will you have to put into remodeling or redecorating the property, and how long will it take to complete the project? Factor that into your offer. A good strategy is to offer an amount that is close to the asking price, but a rate of interest that is below market interest for the first six months, and slightly higher for the second six months. This should give you the time you need to complete any necessary work and either rent or sell the house.

A Scenario

In the early 1990s, as the savings and loan boom busted and financial institutions crashed, a virtual flood of foreclosures appeared in the oil states—Texas, Alaska, Colorado, Oklahoma, Kansas, and parts of California. Those lenders left standing had to hire whole new REO departments so that resales could be made as quickly as possible.

A friend of mine from San Diego was quick to recognize the opportunity, and bought several foreclosed properties in Colorado and southern California. In each instance, he bargained hard on the price and harder on the interest rate. In Colorado, for instance, my friend was able to purchase a warehouse from the lender for about 60 percent of the property's original cost. Moreover, he secured an interest rate of prime plus .5 percent, with no personal liability for two years. After that, the interest would rise to market rates.

The warehouse required little work, but the residential unit on the roof needed refurbishing, and the entire property required cleaning and painting. My friend completed all the work, improving the landscaping, fixing the parking lots, and filling the holes in the stucco. Finally, he put up a large "For Lease" banner. Within six months, a printing company was occupying the warehouse, and the penthouse was rented to one of the company's salesmen.

Refinancing Old Property to Purchase New Property

When interest rates drop, property owners in general, and homeowners in particular, are presented with a unique opportunity: The chance to refinance by replacing their old high-interest loan with a new low-interest loan. There are several reasons to refinance. Refinancing can lower your monthly mortgage payment, can replace your adjustable-rate mortgage with a fixed-rate mortgage, or can shorten the number of years on your loan. If you're a real estate investor, though, refinancing has special appeal, as it can enable you to take the cash from some of the equity you've acquired and purchase new real estate for either short-term profit or long-term investment goals.

The Strategy

You have lived in your home for many years, and have a good deal of equity in it. Yet you're still paying a high rate of interest on your mortgage. Meanwhile, interest rates have dropped. Although you own other properties, you know that the home market has the lowest interest rates and the least complicated and expensive loan costs. Therefore, you decide to look into refinancing your home, and using the resulting capital to buy investment property.

First, approach a real estate agent and get a ballpark idea of your home's worth by requesting a *broker's opinion of value*, or

BOV. A BOV is generally free, and although it will not satisfy a lender, it will enable you to estimate the amount of money that may be available to you if you refinance. Take the BOV, and subtract from it your present mortgage balance, plus the brokerage fees and sales costs that would be incurred if you were to sell your property. The remaining sum is your likely cash equity.

Generally, lenders will be willing to make a loan of from 75 to 90 percent of the fair market value of your home. However, a number of factors will also come into play, including whether this is your primary residence, vacation home, or rental; the available amortization period; the interest rate offered; and, of course, your current equity in the property. The loan specialist at your local lender will be able to provide an accurate figure.

After you find a new property that fits your parameters, make an offer subject to acquiring a loan. When the offer is accepted, follow the steps necessary to refinance your old property. The money you receive should be adequate to cover the down payment on your new investment.

A Scenario

A friend had purchased his home for $105,000, with the seller carrying back the note and mortgage. My friend worked long hours, and over the next twenty years, he paid little attention to his property's growing value. When he began to think seriously of his eventual retirement, however, he decided to get a broker's opinion of value on his house, and learned that it was now worth roughly $265,000. After subtracting the remaining mortgage balance plus closing fees, he realized that he had about $215,000 of equity in his home.

After making a quick tour of local lenders, my friend found that he could borrow 75 percent of the home's value, with an interest rate of 8.5 percent and a term of thirty years. After loan costs, that would leave him $155,000.

After shopping around, my friend decided to use his newfound cash to buy a four-plex. He bought the property for $385,000 with $150,000 down, and a loan of $235,000 amortizing over thirty years. To derive the maximum benefits from his investment, he moved into one of the four-plex's three-bedroom units. He then rented his original house for a sum large enough to cover the new mortgage payment, taxes, insurance, and expected maintenance.

A year and a half later, the value of the four-plex had increased to $415,000. My friend was able to raise the rents, and knew he could look forward to enjoying the increased cash flow throughout his retirement years.

Conclusion

I n my many years of helping clients find and finance real estate purchases, I've discovered that those who take the time to understand the numerous financing strategies available—the very strategies presented in this book—are those who end up with the best portfolios. These are the people who get the bank loan even when money is tight; who buy that great piece of corner property before anyone else even begins to arrange financing; who find a way to take that crumbling commercial building and turn it into a moneymaker. *How to Finance Any Real Estate, Any Place, Any Time* has provided you with the essentials you need to finance property in ways that you may never have known were possible. Now it's time to take what you've learned and put it to use.

First and foremost, put together a group of experienced professionals—an attorney, accountant, and escrow closer—who are just as excited about the challenge of the real estate market as you are. Then look for a good piece of property, and determine which strategy will enable you to complete the transaction. Keep in mind that the sellers with whom you're working may be unfamiliar with these strategies, and may be hesitant to approach real estate transactions in a new way. Your job is to point out the benefits they will enjoy as the result of the strategy. As I mentioned early on, one of the keys to successfully financing real estate deals is to determine the benefits for which everyone is looking, and find a strategy that provides them with what they want, whether it's immediate cash or a steady stream of income. As long as you select the right technique and explain its advantages, you have an excellent chance of closing the deal.

I have collected, developed, and refined these financing strategies over three decades. As you use these strategies, I hope that you learn to modify and adapt them to meet the needs of each individual investment, just as I have learned to fine-tune the same strategies to suit different economic climates, different properties, and different players. Deals are not made in a textbook, but in the real world with real people. That's why the same strategy—using an option, for instance—may be employed in various ways in various circumstances. So don't be afraid to put your own spin on an old strategy or to combine strategies as a means of persuading a hesitant lender to make a loan, or encouraging a reluctant seller to go to contract.

One last thought: It doesn't take a real estate professional to devise a great new financing technique. Through the years, I've gotten nearly as many valuable ideas from clients as I have from fellow realtors and investors! If you do develop any new and effective strategies, I'd love to hear about them and share them with other readers in future editions of this book. Please send your suggestions to:

Att: How to Finance
Square One Publishers
115 Herricks Road
Garden City Park, NY 11040

Appendices

Glossary

All words that appear in *italic type* are defined within the glossary.

abstract of title. A historical summary of a property's *title* that goes back to the first owner. This type of title report—used mainly in the so-called abstract states found on the East Coast and in the Midwest—is prepared by the buyer's attorney.

adjusted basis. The original cost of any property, whether raw or improved, lowered by *depreciation* and raised by *capital improvements.* See also *cost basis.*

agreement of sale. See *contract of sale.*

amortization. The paying off of a debt over a period of time through installment payments that include both interest and principal.

annuity. Any investment that generates a series of regular payments guaranteed to continue for a specified period of time.

appraisal. 1. An estimation of a property's value given by a qualified individual, usually after a property inspection. **2.** The report that sets forth the process of estimation and conclusion of value.

appreciation. The increase in a property's value due to a number of factors, including *inflation,* decreased taxes, an increased demand for land or housing, and modernization of the property itself or of the surrounding neighborhood.

asking price. The list price that the seller would like to receive for a property.

assessed value. The value established for a property by the county assessor for property tax purposes. This may be higher or lower than *market value.*

asset-based mortgage. See *chattel mortgage.*

attach. To take a person's property into legal custody in order to force payment of a debt.

balloon payment. A loan payment that is greater than the installment payments that preceded it and that reduces the loan, sometimes paying the loan in full.

binder. A preliminary agreement, accompanied by a deposit, for the purchase of real estate as evidence of the buyer's intention to complete the transaction.

blanket mortgage. A single *mortgage* that covers more than one piece of property.

BOV. See *broker's opinion of value.*

bridge loan. A short-term loan for borrowers who need time to secure permanent financing. The bridge loan therefore "bridges" the gap between the end of one loan and the beginning of another loan, or between the purchase of a piece of property and the acquisition of a conventional mortgage. This is also called a swing loan.

broker's opinion of value (BOV). A real estate broker's determination of the *market value* of a property. Note that this is not an official *appraisal,* but only an opinion.

C corporation. A *corporation* that is a separate taxable entity, meaning that the profits and losses are taxed directly to the corporation at a corporate income tax rate. Distributions made to shareholders are then taxed at the rate of the individual shareholders. See also *S corporation.*

capital asset. A long-term asset, such as raw or improved property, that is not bought or sold in the normal course of business.

capital gain. The amount by which the sale price of a *capital asset* exceeds its *adjusted basis.*

capital improvement. An improvement to a property that will have a life of more than one year, and will generally be depreciated over its useful life.

cash flow. The periodic income available to an investor after all periodic expenses, including the *mortgage* debt, have been paid. For instance, the cash flow of a rental apartment would be computed by subtracting expenditures such as taxes, utilities, and mortgage payments (the money going out) from the rent (the money coming in).

cash-on-cash return. A measure of the profitability of an income-producing property, expressed as a percentage. To calculate the cash-on-cash return of an investment, divide the amount of cash received from the property in a given year by the amount originally invested.

certificate of deposit (CD). A type of savings account in which a specified sum of money is deposited for a set period of time, yielding a return that is generally higher than that of a passbook-type savings account.

chattel mortgage. A pledge of personal property—a car, boat, or livestock, for instance—as security for a debt. This is sometimes referred to as an asset-based mortgage.

closing. The event that transfers ownership of a property from the seller to the buyer in accordance with the *contract of sale*. Generally, the buyer, seller, lender (if any), and their agents are present at the closing.

collateral. Property pledged as security for a debt. If the debt is not repaid in accordance with the terms of the *security instrument*—the *mortgage* or *deed of trust*—the borrower risks losing the property.

collateral security. Additional security supplied by a borrower to obtain a loan. This security may be in the form of personal property such as a car or boat, or may be *paper*, such as promissory notes, stocks, or bonds. The property is not given to the seller but, instead, is pledged to the seller so that if the buyer defaults on his payments, the seller can take possession of the property and either keep it or sell it to cover damages.

commercial property. Real estate intended for use by a retail, wholesale, office, hotel, or service business. Properties deemed commercial include hotels and motels, apartment houses, resorts, restaurants, service stations, convenience stores, shopping centers, and office buildings.

compound interest. *Interest* paid on both the *principal* and any unpaid accumulated interest of previous periods. See also *simple interest.*

condominium. An individual unit in a multi-unit attached residential or commercial structure, in which the individual units are owned privately, and any commonly used areas such as sidewalks are owned jointly.

consideration. Anything of value given to induce someone to enter into a contract, such as an *option* or a *land lease.* The consideration can be cash or other personal property, or can be personal services.

contract of sale. A written agreement between the buyer and the owner of a piece of property, in which the buyer agrees to buy the property and the owner agrees to sell as long as certain conditions are satisfied. This is also called an agreement of sale and a purchase agreement.

contract rent. The rent of a unit such as an apartment as stated in the contract. See also *market rent.*

corporation. A state-chartered business or organization formed by a group of people, and having rights and liabilities separate from those of the individuals involved. The corporation is characterized by the limited liability of its owners; the issuance of freely transferable shares; centralized management; and the fact that it can exist indefinitely, beyond the lifetimes of any members or founders. See also *C corporation; S corporation.*

cost basis. The original cost of any property, whether raw or improved. See also *adjusted basis.*

decreasing term life insurance. A life insurance policy that reduces the lump sum paid at death over the term of the plan. This policy is often used when the financial needs of the policyholder are expected to decrease over time.

deed of trust. A legal document, used in states west of the Mississippi instead of a *mortgage,* that pledges property to secure the repayment of a loan. A deed of trust vests the *title* of the property in one or several trustees to secure the loan's payment. This is also called a trust deed.

defect in title. Any recorded legal document, such as a *lien,* that makes the ownership of a property subject to a competing claim.

delayed exchange. See *Starker exchange.*

depreciation. The lessening of a property's value over time due to wear or *obsolescence.*

depreciation allowance. The amount that an owner of *improved land* can deduct from his taxable income each year based on the structure's perceived loss of value due to age and wear and tear. This allowance partly depends on whether the property is residential or commercial.

developed land. See *improved land.*

developer. An individual or company that makes a business of transforming *raw land* into *improved land* through the use of capital and labor.

discount. The difference between the current balance of a promissory *note* or other obligation and the amount actually paid for the note.

discount points. See *points.*

discounted note. A promissory *note* sold for less than its current balance.

discretionary funds. Any money that remains from net income after essential living expenses have been paid.

down payment. The portion of the purchase price of a property that the buyer pays in cash or exchange equity rather than financing with a *mortgage.*

due diligence. A careful study performed of the physical, financial, legal, and social characteristics of a specific piece of property, and of its projected investment performance.

duplex. 1. A building that contains two living units. **2.** An apartment that has rooms on two floors.

earnest money deposit. A deposit made by a buyer of real estate, generally at the signing of the contract, to show serious intent to purchase the property and to make the contract legally binding.

encumbrance. Anything, such as a *mortgage* or tax, that complicates the title process and affects the value or use of a property.

equity. The interest or value that an owner has in property over and above any existing debt.

equity investor. An individual who has purchased partial ownership of a property by supplying cash rather than expertise.

escrow. Money deposited with a third party, called an *escrow agent,* to be delivered upon the fulfillment of conditions stipulated in a *contract of sale.*

escrow agent. An individual or company that receives *escrow* for deposit or delivery. In some states, the *title insurance company* most often serves as the escrow agent. In other states, an attorney typically holds the escrow.

face value. 1. The value of a promissory *note* at its creation. See also *note balance.* **2.** The amount that the issuer of a *zero coupon bond* agrees to pay when the bond reaches maturity.

fair market value. See *market value.*

foreclosure. The legal process whereby a borrower who has failed to make *mortgage* payments is deprived of his ownership interest in the mortgaged property. This usually involves a forced sale of the property, the proceeds of which are used to pay the mortgage debt.

foreclosure sale. The public sale of a mortgaged property following *foreclosure.* The proceeds of the sale are used to pay the *mortgage* debt, with any excess going to the mortgagor (the property owner).

four-plex. A building that contains four living units.

handyman's special. A house that requires extensive remodeling and repairs, and, as a result, sells for a relatively low price.

hard equity. A contribution to the construction of property in the form of cash rather than labor or services. See also *soft equity.*

improved land. Land that has been partly or fully developed for use through the addition of utilities, landscaping, roads, or buildings. This is also known as developed land.

Individual Retirement Account (IRA). A personal retirement account that an individual can establish by making yearly contributions which are limited in amount. Various types of IRAs are available, each with its own rules. See also *Roth IRA; traditional IRA.*

inflation. 1. An increase in price levels. **2.** A loss in the purchasing power of money.

infrastructure. Basic public works such as roads, sewers, water systems, drainage systems, and utilities.

interest. The cost of borrowing or otherwise using money, expressed as a rate, such as 6 percent. Depending on the way it is calculated, interest can be either simple or compound. See *compound interest; simple interest.*

IRA. See *Individual Retirement Account.*

IRA administrator. In this book, a company that has full responsibility for the operation of a *self-directed IRA.* The administrator reviews the documentation of each investment vehicle; compiles the paperwork necessary for each transaction; files the paperwork with the IRS; and holds cash, *title* to properties, and all other assets of the account.

judgment. The verdict of a court in a civil action, stating that one individual is indebted to another, and fixing the amount of the debt. For instance, if a renter fails to pay rent, the landlord can obtain a judgment from the court against the renter.

judgment creditor. The legal entity—an individual or a company—that has received a *judgment* for money due from a *judgment debtor.*

judgment debtor. The legal entity—an individual or a company—against which a *judgment* has been issued.

land lease. A rental agreement that allows a nonowner to use land in a manner acceptable to both parties.

land sale contract. A legal document, used in some areas of the Midwest and West instead of a *mortgage,* which passes the ownership (*title*) of a property to the buyer only after the contract has been paid in full. This is also called a real estate contract.

lease. A contract by which a property owner (a *lessor* or landlord) permits another party (a *lessee* or tenant) to occupy part or all of the property in exchange for rent payments. The lease contract specifies the premises to be rented, the amount to be paid, the payment period, and other rights and obligations of the lessor and lessee.

lease with option to purchase. A *lease* that gives the tenant the right to purchase the rented property at an agreed-upon price after having paid rent for a specified period of time.

leaseback. An arrangement whereby a piece of property is simultaneously sold and leased back to the seller, usually for long-term use.

lender. A person, lending institution, or government agency that makes a real property loan, or any assignee or transferee, in whole or in part, of such a person or agency.

lessee. The person to whom property is rented under a *lease*. A tenant.

lessor. The person who rents property to another under a *lease*. A landlord.

leverage. The use of borrowed money to increase investment power.

lien. A legal claim that one person has on the property of another person as security for a debt. A *mortgage*, for example, is considered a lien.

life estate. An agreement whereby the owner of a piece of property transfers title to another individual or to an organization, while retaining the right to occupy and otherwise enjoy full use of the property for either a term of years or the lifetime of one or more individuals, such as the owner and his spouse.

limited liability company (LLC). A combination of a *corporation* and a partnership in which each party buys shares in a property according to the funds he has available. Like a corporation, the LLC offers personal liability to each of the parties involved so that members can't lose more money than they contributed. Like a partnership, earnings are taxed only once.

limited partnership. A form of ownership in which there are two types of partners: limited partners and general partners. Limited partners provide financial backing, but have no role in the management of the property and no personal liability for its debts. General partners are responsible for managing the property, and have unlimited personal liability. Like *limited liability companies*, limited partnerships allow each party to buy units in a property according to the funds he has available.

list price. See *asking price.*

LLC. See *limited liability company.*

loan discounts. See *points.*

loan origination fees. See *points.*

loan-to-value ratio (LTV). The relationship between the amount of money borrowed on a property and the value of the property. A loan with a lower loan-to-value ratio—in other words, a loan in which the amount borrowed is smaller relative to the property's value—has more value than a loan with a higher ratio, because the borrower has more *equity* in the property, and therefore more reason to repay the loan.

manufactured home. See *mobile home.*

market price. The actual price paid for a piece of property. Note that this is different from *market value.*

market rent. The rent that a comparable rental unit—a similar house, for instance—would command if offered on the market. See also *contract rent.*

market value. An estimation of the price that could be obtained for a piece of property on the current market. This is sometimes referred to as fair market value.

maximum loan charges. See *points.*

mobile home. A residential unit manufactured in a factory and designed for transport to a permanent site, such as a mobile home park or a mobile home subdivision. This is also known as a manufactured home.

money market account. A type of savings account that invests funds in money market instruments, such as United States Treasury bills, *certificates of deposit,* and commercial *paper.*

mortgage. A legal document that pledges property to a lender as security for payment of a debt. For the most part, the mortgage is used only in states east of the Mississippi. In other states, a *deed of trust* or *land sale contract* is more prevalent.

mortgage back. See *owner financing.*

mortgage cancellation insurance. A form of insurance that pays off a mortgage holder in the event of the homeowner's death. This is also known as personal mortgage insurance (PMI).

net lease. A lease in which the tenants pay such expenses as taxes, insurance, and maintenance. See also *triple-net lease.*

nonrecourse loan. A type of loan structured so that if the loan isn't paid back as promised, the lender may take only the property to satisfy the debt, and may not take any of the borrower's other assets, such as his car.

note. A legal document that obligates the borrower to repay a debt, such as a *mortgage* loan, at a stated *interest* rate during a specified period of time. This is also called a promissory note.

note balance. The amount remaining to be paid on a promissory *note*. See also *face value*.

obsolescence. Loss of a property's value due to the structure's becoming outmoded in design, style, or construction.

offer. A verbal or written statement of the buyer's interest in purchasing a property at a specified price and terms. A verbal offer is never legally binding. In most states, however, a written offer accompanied by *consideration* is binding.

one-hundred-percent location. A site that is far superior to other sites in the area due to a commanding view, unusually good access, or other factors. Because it's the "best" site, land values and rents are normally highest in that area.

option. A written, recordable right to purchase a property under specified conditions, within a specified period of time.

option consideration. Cash or other property given to an owner to secure an *option* to purchase his property.

ordinary income. Income other than capital gains. Examples of ordinary income include wages, interest, dividends, and net income from a business.

owner financing. Financing provided by the owner (seller) of a property, rather than by a conventional lender such as a bank. The owner, in essence, assumes the role of the banker, and carries back the loan in the form of a note. The buyer then makes regular payments to the seller, typically on a monthly basis, until the loan is paid off. This is also called seller financing, seller carry-back, vendor take-back mortgage, and mortgage back.

paper. A written obligation, such as a *note, mortgage, contract of sale,* or *deed of trust,* that is backed by property.

pass-through taxation. A form of taxation—characteristic of *S corporations, limited partnerships,* and *limited liability companies*—whereby the income or loss generated by the business passes through to the shareholders, partners, or members for use on their respective income tax returns.

path of progress. An area toward which development and industry are moving. For instance, a vacant lot that is said to be "in the path of progress" may be near the exit ramp of a soon-to-be-built highway, or adjacent to the site of an upcoming shopping center. Property that's in the path of progress can usually be expected to increase in value.

personal mortgage insurance (PMI). See *mortgage cancellation insurance.*

points. Loan fees charged by mortgage lenders. Each point equals one percent of the loan principal. Points are also called discount points, loan discounts, loan origination fees, and maximum loan charges.

principal. 1. The amount of money to be paid back on a *mortgage* or other loan, as opposed to the *interest* paid on it. **2.** The capital or main body of a financial holding. **3.** The owner of a property or a legal entity.

promissory note. See *note.*

property tax. A government-imposed tax based on the *assessed value* of privately owned real estate. This is also called real estate tax.

purchase agreement. See *contract of sale.*

raw land. Land that has no improvements such as utilities, landscaping, roads, drainage, and buildings. See also *improved land.*

real estate contract. See *land sale contract.*

real estate tax. See *property tax.*

real property loan. A loan, mortgage, advance, or credit sale secured by a lien on real property.

refinance. To replace an old loan with a new loan.

replacement cost. The total cost of constructing a building that would replace or serve the function of the existing structure. The replacement cost is likely to be greater than the *market value.*

Roth IRA. A type of *Individual Retirement Account* in which money is taxed the year it is contributed. Any gain, however, is not subject to income tax the year it is withdrawn. See also *traditional IRA.*

S corporation. A *corporation* that has *pass-through taxation,* meaning that the income or loss generated by the corporation passes through to individual shareholders for use on their respective income tax returns.

secured loan. A loan that is backed by *collateral,* such as real estate.

security instrument. An interest in real estate that allows the involved property to be sold in the event of failure to fulfill an obligation or promise. A security instrument is more specifically called a *deed of trust* or *mortgage.*

self-directed IRA. An *Individual Retirement Account* whose administrator permits the account holder to choose the vehicles in which his funds are invested. These vehicles may include real estate, mutual funds, stocks and bonds, and other investments approved by the Internal Revenue Service. Any type of IRA—including *traditional IRAs* and *Roth IRAs*—can be self-directed.

seller carry-back. See *owner financing.*

seller financing. See *owner financing.*

sickness and accident insurance. A type of insurance that guarantees a degree of replacement income in the event that sickness or accident makes the policyholder unable to work, and therefore causes his regular income to cease.

simple interest. Interest paid only on the *principal,* and not on any accumulated interest. See also *compound interest.*

soft equity. A contribution to the construction of property in the form of labor or services rather than cash. This is also called sweat equity. See also *hard equity.*

soft market. A market in which demand has shrunk or supply has exceeded demand, causing prices to fall.

soft paper. *Paper* with lower-than-market interest rates and long-term payments.

spec house. A single-family house built in anticipation of finding a buyer. The builder "speculates" that a buyer will be found.

Starker exchange. A transaction in which a property is traded for the promise to provide a replacement property in the near future. Several strict requirements must be met. This is also referred to as a Starker transaction or a delayed exchange.

Starker transaction. See *Starker exchange.*

stripped bond. See *zero coupon bond.*

subdivision. A large parcel of land that's divided into individual lots, each of which is suitable for the building of a house or commercial building.

sweat equity. See *soft equity.*

swing loan. See *bridge loan.*

syndication. A method of buying property whereby a syndicator—a sponsor, in other words—sells interests to other investors. The syndication can take various forms, including that of a *limited partnership, a limited liability company,* or a *corporation.*

tax lien. A legal claim placed on a property due to failure to pay property taxes.

tax roll. A list of all properties subject to taxation in a county or other jurisdiction. Among other facts, the list includes the *assessed value* of each property and the name of the property's owner.

tax sale. The sale of a property due to nonpayment of taxes.

tax sale certificate. A certificate sold by a county or other taxing unit when the owner of real estate is delinquent in paying his property taxes to the point that *foreclosure* is imminent. A tax sale certificate gives the buyer the right to collect lawful interest; to give proper notices to foreclose; to obtain possession of the property by court eviction; and to reside in, lease, rent, or dispose of the property at will.

term. 1. The period of time during which something, such as a loan, is in effect. **2.** A condition specified in a legal agreement.

title. 1. The rights of ownership and possession of a particular property. **2.** The legal document that establishes the rights of ownership.

title insurance. A policy that protects the holder from any losses sustained by recorded *defects in title*—in other words, against competing claims to a property's ownership. Items that are unrecorded or the result of faulty surveys are covered only by an American Land Title Association (ALTA) policy.

title insurance company. A corporation that performs *title searches* and sells policies of insurance that guarantee the *title* to a property.

title report. A document that indicates the current status of a property's *title*, but offers no protection until the premium is paid and a certificate of insurance is issued. See also *title search.*

title search. The process of examining public records that relate to the ownership of a property to insure that the current owner has clear *title*, free of any *liens* or competing claims. The title search may be performed by an attorney, *title insurance company*, or other qualified title searcher, usually on behalf of the proposed purchaser of the property. In some states, found mostly on the East Coast and in the Midwest, the buyer's attorney prepares an *abstract of title*, which is a historical summary of the property's title that goes back to the first owner. In other states, typically found on the West Coast and in the Rocky Mountain region, the title company researches the property only to the last time the title was issued.

traditional IRA. The most common type of *Individual Retirement Account*, in which money is tax-deductible the year it is contributed, but subject to income tax the year it is withdrawn. See also *Roth IRA.*

triple-net lease. A lease in which the tenants pay all of the property's operating costs, including utilities, taxes, maintenance, and insurance. The owner, then, receives a net rent. See also *net lease.*

trust. A legal entity created by the owner of property for the purpose of administering and distributing such property for the benefit of the owner and/or other persons, known as beneficiaries.

trust deed. See *deed of trust.*

vendor take-back mortgage. See *owner financing.*

wraparound mortgage. A creative financing tool that combines an existing *mortgage* with a new loan, resulting in an interest rate that is somewhere between the old rate and the current market rate.

yield. The return earned on an investment.

zero coupon bond. A bond that has no coupons and pays no interest during the life of the bond, but is purchased at a fraction of its *face value* and, through the accrual of interest, pays its face value at maturity. This bond is also known as a stripped bond, because interest coupons have been stripped away.

Resource List

Now that you've learned so many ways to finance real estate ventures, you may wish to start looking for properties, learning more about real estate trends, or otherwise polishing your investment skills. The groups and websites listed below can help you easily locate the information you need.

CCIM Institute
Website: www.ccim.com

The website of the CCIM Institute enables you to search for a CCIM (Certified Commercial Investment Member) by market area, property type, and specialization; or by city. Each member is a recognized professional in commercial real estate. CCIM also offers comprehensive courses in commercial real estate.

GlobeSt.com
520 Eighth Avenue, Fl. 17
New York, NY 10018
Phone: 212-929-6900
Website: www.globest.com

This free online newsletter provides information on real estate and market conditions around the globe. Links connect you to an online bookstore, listings of real estate conferences, and more.

Inman News

Website: www.inman.com/index.asp

This independent news service provides commercial real estate information for both consumers and real estate professionals. A number of articles are available on the Inman website to nonmembers. A weekly print newsletter, a database of articles, and other services are available to members only.

LoopNet

185 Berry Street, Suite 4000

San Francisco, CA 94107

Phone: 415-243-4200

Website: www.loopnet.com

Designed to serve the local and national needs of the commercial real estate industry, LoopNet provides an online listing of more than 220,000 commercial properties for lease and sale. Listings and other services are available to members only, but membership is available to anyone who's interested.

MapQuest

Website: www.mapquest.com

This useful website provides written driving instructions and detailed maps to help you find any property of interest. Other online tools include a Road Trip Planner for extended trips and extensive Yellow Page listings.

Moreover Technologies, Inc.

330 Pine Street

San Francisco, CA 94104

Phone: 415-989-0600

Website: www.moreover.com

Moreover gathers real estate news from Internet sources and e-mails it to clients, tailoring the news to each customer's specific business needs.

NAREIT
1875 Eye Street, NW
Washington, DC 20006
Phone: 202-739-9400
Website: www.nareit.com/home.cfm

The National Association of Real Estate Investment Trusts (NAREIT) is the trade association for REITS and publicly traded real estate companies. Nonmembers are eligible for some educational and networking resources, but numerous services—such as a continually updated online directory of corporate members, a bimonthly magazine called *Real Estate Portfolio*, and access to current industry research information—are available to members only.

PikeNet
Box 1177
Ross, CA 94957
Phone: 415-485-6700
Website: www.pikenet.com

The PikeNet online directory of commercial real estate offers almost 3,500 links to real estate resources and service providers worldwide, from exchange services to auctions to foreclosure listings. Use of the directory is made easy by a search feature. PikeNet also produces a free online newsletter, *The PikeNet Dispatch*, which is designed to increase the productivity of real estate practitioners and report on business trends, marketing strategies, and technology tools.

Property Exchange Registry (Propxchange)
Phone: 619-224-8584
Website: www.propxchange.com

This website enables property owners, sellers, exchangors, and brokers to list and find a variety of commercial and investment properties, as well as condos and single-family houses. Although most properties are located in California, real estate in other areas of the country is listed as well. The website also enables you to request referrals whenever professional advice is needed.

Real Estate Cyberspace Society (RECS)
189 Wells Avenue, 3rd Floor
Newton, MA 02459
Phone: 617-559-0002
Website: www.recyber.com

RECS put you in touch with all aspects of investment real estate technology. The society, which is worldwide, provides the names and locations of its members—all of whom are real estate professionals—and presents the members' properties. Sections include residential, commercial-investment, auction, historical, and more.

Real Estate Exchange.com
PO Box 1450
McCall, ID 83638
Phone: 208-634-2999
Website: www.ree.com

In addition to providing listings of properties for exchange or sale, Real Estate Exchange.com offers information on a variety of important topics, as well as creative solutions to numerous real estate problems.

Real Estate Journal
Website: www.realestatejournal.com

Produced by *The Wall Street Journal*, *Real Estate Journal* is an online guide to buying, selling, and maintaining a home. Articles cover a variety of topics, including mortgages, taxes, and second homes. A link leads you to property and estate listings.

Real Estate Research Corporation (RERC)
980 North Michigan Avenue, Suite 1675
Chicago, IL 60611
Phone: 312-587-1800
Website: www.rerc.com

RERC is one of the most recognized commercial real estate research, valuation, and consulting firms in the nation. With clients ranging from lending institutions to individual real estate investors, the Real Estate Research Corporation serves its members by providing research, publications, market studies, property valuations, investment criteria, and trends and analysis.

ReExchange

Website: www.reexchange.com

Designed to assist investors who wish to sell, buy, or exchange real estate, this information exchange allows you to list your own properties, view hundreds of properties, get lists of verified buyers and sellers, and correspond with buyers and sellers.

Reis, Inc.

5 West 37th Street

New York, NY 10018

Phone: 212-921-1122

Website: www.reis.com

This website provides timely information about real estate trends around the nation. Articles are offered free of charge, but information on comparable sales, property valuations, etc., is available to subscribers only.

The Society of Exchange Counselors

5580 La Jolla Boulevard #110

La Jolla, CA 92037

Phone: 858-488-3750

Website: www.secounselors.com

www.secedfoundation.com

With members that include real estate brokers, investors, counselors, developers, asset managers, financiers, exchangors, consultants, and educators, this national organization is committed to practicing creative real estate and counseling. Through its affiliate, the SEC Education Foundation, SEC provides a variety of educational programs, as well as an online publication, the *SEC Real Estate Observer* (www.secobserver.com).

Xceligent, Inc.

4231 S. Hocker Drive

Independence, MO 64055

Phone: 877-628-5300

Website: www.xceligent.com

Xceligent offers members an extensive database of commercial property information, and will develop a customized database to meet a client's unique needs.

Selected IRA Trustees and Custodians

In Strategy 43, you learned that if you want to use funds from your IRA to purchase real estate, you need to have an experienced IRA administrator that can assist you in making investments through a self-directed retirement plan. For simplicity, I used the term "administrator" in Strategy 43; however, you actually need a trustee or custodian with administrative capabilities. The following list includes a select group of companies that have proven to be exceptionally skilled and flexible.

American Church Trust Company
14615 Benfer Road
Houston, TX 77069
Phone: 800-228-8825
Website:
    www.churchtrust.com

CNA Trust Corporation
3080 South Bristol Street,
    2nd Floor
Costa Mesa, CA 92626
Phone: 800-274-8798
Website: www.cnatrust.com

First Trust Corporation
Phone: 800-525-2124
Website: www.firsttrust.com

Lincoln Trust
PO Box 5831
Denver, CO 80217
Phone: 800-825-2501
Website: www.lincolntrust.com

PENSCO Trust Company
250 Montgomery Street,
    3rd Floor
San Francisco, CA 94104
Phone: 800-969-4472
Website: www.pensco.com

Sterling Trust Company
PO Box 2526
Waco, TX 76702
Phone: 800-955-3434
Website: www.sterling-trust.com

The Internal Revenue Service Code on Property Exchanges

Title 26—Internal Revenue Code
Section 1031. Nontaxable Exchanges

The tax strategies inset on page 21, as well as Strategy 7 on page 27, describe the Starker exchange—a means by which you can exchange one property for another *without paying capital gains tax.* This exchange is a great financing tool because by saving you money in taxes, it will make more money available for your real estate investments. However, if you've read those earlier discussions, you know that in order to avoid a taxable event, you must stick to the rules laid down by the IRS. Below, these rules have been presented in full so that you and the professionals that assist you will be better able to structure tax-smart real estate exchanges.

TITLE 26 - INTERNAL REVENUE CODE
Subtitle A - Income Taxes
CHAPTER 1 - NORMAL TAXES AND SURTAXES
Subchapter O - Gain or Loss on Disposition of Property
PART III - COMMON NONTAXABLE EXCHANGES
-HEAD-
    Sec. 1031. Exchange of property held for productive use or
        investment
-STATUTE-
    (a) Nonrecognition of gain or loss from exchanges solely in kind

(1) In general

No gain or loss shall be recognized on the exchange of property held for productive use in a trade or business or for investment if such property is exchanged solely for property of like kind which is to be held either for productive use in a trade or business or for investment.

(2) Exception

This subsection shall not apply to any exchange of -

(A) stock in trade or other property held primarily for sale,

(B) stocks, bonds, or notes,

(C) other securities or evidences of indebtedness or interest,

(D) interests in a partnership,

(E) certificates of trust or beneficial interests, or

(F) choses in action.

For purposes of this section, an interest in a partnership which has in effect a valid election under section 761(a) to be excluded from the application of all of subchapter K shall be treated as an interest in each of the assets of such partnership and not as an interest in a partnership.

(3) Requirement that property be identified and that exchange be completed not more than 180 days after transfer of exchanged property

For purposes of this subsection, any property received by the taxpayer shall be treated as property which is not like-kind property if -

(A) such property is not identified as property to be received in the exchange on or before the day which is 45 days after the date on which the taxpayer transfers the property relinquished in the exchange, or

(B) such property is received after the earlier of -

(i) the day which is 180 days after the date on which the taxpayer transfers the property relinquished in the exchange, or

(ii) the due date (determined with regard to extension) for the transferor's return of the tax imposed by this chapter for the taxable year in which the transfer of the relinquished property occurs.

(b) Gain from exchanges not solely in kind

If an exchange would be within the provisions of subsection (a), of section 1035(a), of section 1036(a), or of section 1037(a), if it were not for the fact that the property received in exchange consists not only of property permitted by such provisions to be received without the recognition of gain, but also of other property or money, then the gain, if any, to the recipient shall be recognized, but in an amount not in excess of the sum of such money and the fair market value of such other property.

(c) Loss from exchanges not solely in kind

If an exchange would be within the provisions of subsection (a), of section 1035(a), of section 1036(a), or of section 1037(a), if it were not for the fact that the property received in exchange consists not only of property permitted by such provisions to be received without the recognition of gain or loss, but also of other property or money, then no loss from the exchange shall be recognized.

(d) Basis

If property was acquired on an exchange described in this section, section 1035(a), section 1036(a), or section 1037(a), then the basis shall be the same as that of the property exchanged, decreased in the amount of any money received by the taxpayer and increased in the amount of gain or decreased in the amount of loss to the taxpayer that was recognized on such exchange. If the property so acquired consisted in part of the type of property permitted by this section, section 1035(a), section 1036(a), or section 1037(a), to be received without the recognition of gain or loss, and in part of other property, the basis provided in this subsection shall be allocated between the properties (other than money) received, and for the purpose of the allocation there shall be assigned to such other property an amount equivalent to its fair market value at the date of the exchange. For purposes of this section, section 1035(a), and section 1036(a), where as part of the consideration to the taxpayer another party to the exchange assumed (as determined under section 357(d)) a liability of the taxpayer, such assumption shall be considered as money received by the taxpayer on the exchange.

(e) Exchanges of livestock of different sexes

For purposes of this section, livestock of different sexes are not property of a like kind.

(f) Special rules for exchanges between related persons

(1) In general

If -

(A) a taxpayer exchanges property with a related person,

(B) there is nonrecognition of gain or loss to the taxpayer under this section with respect to the exchange of such property (determined without regard to this subsection), and

(C) before the date 2 years after the date of the last transfer which was part of such exchange -

(i) the related person disposes of such property, or

(ii) the taxpayer disposes of the property received in the exchange from the related person which was of like kind to the property transferred by the taxpayer,

there shall be no nonrecognition of gain or loss under this section to the taxpayer with respect to such exchange; except that any gain or loss recognized by the taxpayer by reason of this subsection shall be taken into account as of the date on which the disposition referred to in subparagraph (C) occurs.

(2) Certain dispositions not taken into account

For purposes of paragraph (1)(C), there shall not be taken into account any disposition -

(A) after the earlier of the death of the taxpayer or the death of the related person,

(B) in a compulsory or involuntary conversion (within the meaning of section 1033) if the exchange occurred before the threat or imminence of such conversion, or

(C) with respect to which it is established to the satisfaction of the Secretary that neither the exchange nor such disposition had as one of its principal purposes the avoidance of Federal income tax.

(3) Related person

For purposes of this subsection, the term "related person" means any person bearing a relationship to the taxpayer described in section 267(b) or 707(b)(1).

(4) Treatment of certain transactions

This section shall not apply to any exchange which is part of a transaction (or series of transactions) structured to avoid the purposes of this subsection.

(g) Special rule where substantial diminution of risk

(1) In general

If paragraph (2) applies to any property for any period, the running of the period set forth in subsection (f)(1)(C) with respect to such property shall be suspended during such period.

(2) Property to which subsection applies

This paragraph shall apply to any property for any period

during which the holder's risk of loss with respect to the property is substantially diminished by -

(A) the holding of a put with respect to such property,

(B) the holding by another person of a right to acquire such property, or

(C) a short sale or any other transaction.

(h) Special rules for foreign real and personal property

For purposes of this section -

(1) Real property

Real property located in the United States and real property located outside the United States are not property of a like kind.

(2) Personal property

(A) In general

Personal property used predominantly within the United States and personal property used predominantly outside the United States are not property of a like kind.

(B) Predominant use

Except as provided in subparagraph (FOOTNOTE 1) (C) and (D), the predominant use of any property shall be determined based on -

(FOOTNOTE 1) So in original. Probably should be "subparagraphs".

(i) in the case of the property relinquished in the exchange, the 2-year period ending on the date of such relinquishment, and

(ii) in the case of the property acquired in the exchange, the 2-year period beginning on the date of such acquisition.

(C) Property held for less than 2 years

Except in the case of an exchange which is part of a transaction (or series of transactions) structured to avoid the purposes of this subsection -

(i) only the periods the property was held by the person relinquishing the property (or any related person) shall be taken into account under subparagraph (B)(i), and

(ii) only the periods the property was held by the person acquiring the property (or any related person) shall be taken into account under subparagraph (B)(ii).

(D) Special rule for certain property

Property described in any subparagraph of section 168(g)(4) shall be treated as used predominantly in the United States.

-SOURCE-

(Aug. 16, 1954, ch. 736, 68A Stat. 302; Pub. L. 85-866, title I, Sec. 44, Sept. 2, 1958, 72 Stat. 1641; Pub. L. 86-346, title II, Sec. 201(c)-(e), Sept. 22, 1959, 73 Stat. 624; Pub. L. 91-172, title II, Sec. 212(c)(1), Dec. 30, 1969, 83 Stat. 571; Pub. L. 98-369, div. A, title I, Sec. 77(a), July 18, 1984, 98 Stat. 595; Pub. L. 99-514, title XVIII, Sec. 1805(d), Oct. 22, 1986, 100 Stat. 2810; Pub. L. 101-239, title VII, Sec. 7601(a), Dec. 19, 1989, 103 Stat. 2370; Pub. L. 101-508, title XI, Sec. 11701(h), 11703(d)(1), Nov. 5, 1990, 104 Stat. 1388-508, 1388-517; Pub. L. 105-34, title X, Sec. 1052(a), Aug. 5, 1997, 111 Stat. 940; Pub. L. 106-36, title III, Sec. 3001(c)(2), June 25, 1999, 113 Stat. 183.)

-MISC1-

AMENDMENTS

1999 - Subsec. (d). Pub. L. 106-36, in last sentence, substituted "assumed (as determined under section 357(d)) a liability of the taxpayer" for "assumed a liability of the taxpayer or acquired from the taxpayer property subject to a liability" and struck out "or acquisition (in the amount of the liability)" after "such assumption".

1997 - Subsec. (h). Pub. L. 105-34 amended heading and text of subsec. (h) generally. Prior to amendment, text read as follows: "For purposes of this section, real property located in the United States and real property located outside the United States are not property of a like kind."

1990 - Subsec. (a)(2). Pub. L. 101-508, Sec. 11703(d)(1), inserted at end "For purposes of this section, an interest in a partnership which has in effect a valid election under section 761(a) to be excluded from the application of all of subchapter K shall be treated as an interest in each of the assets of such partnership and not as an interest in a partnership."

Subsec. (f)(3). Pub. L. 101-508, Sec. 11701(h), substituted "section 267(b) or 707(b)(1)" for "section 267(b)".

1989 - Subsecs. (f) to (h). Pub. L. 101-239 added subsecs. (f) to (h).

1986 - Subsec. (a)(3)(A). Pub. L. 99-514 substituted "on or before the day" for "before the day".

1984 - Subsec. (a). Pub. L. 98-369, Sec. 77(a), in amending subsec. generally, designated existing provisions as par. (1), substituted "No gain or loss shall be recognized on the exchange of property held for productive use in a trade or business or for investment if such property is exchanged solely for property of like kind which is to be held either for productive use in a trade or business or for investment" for "No gain or loss shall be recognized if property held for productive use in trade or business or for investment (not including stock in trade or other property held primarily for sale, nor stocks, bonds, notes, choses in action, certificates of trust or beneficial interest, or other securities or evidences of indebtedness or interest) is exchanged solely for property of a like kind to be held either for productive use in trade or business or for investment", and added pars. (2) and (3).

1969 - Subsec. (e). Pub. L. 91-172 added subsec. (e).

1959 - Subsecs. (b) to (d). Pub. L. 86-346 inserted references to section 1037(a) in subsecs. (b) and (c) and in first two sentences of subsec. (d).

1958 - Subsec. (d). Pub. L. 85-866 inserted in first sentence a comma between "exchanged" and "decreased" and "or decreased in the amount of loss", and substituted in second sentence "subsection" for "paragraph".

EFFECTIVE DATE OF 1999 AMENDMENT

Amendment by Pub. L. 106-36 applicable to transfers after Oct. 18, 1998, see section 3001(e) of Pub. L. 106-36, set out as a note under section 351 of this title.

EFFECTIVE DATE OF 1997 AMENDMENT

Section 1052(b) of Pub. L. 105-34 provided that:

"(1) In general. - The amendment made by this section (amending this section) shall apply to transfers after June 8, 1997, in taxable years ending after such date.

"(2) Binding contracts. - The amendment made by this section shall not apply to any transfer pursuant to a written binding contract in effect on June 8, 1997, and at all times thereafter before the disposition of property. A contract shall not fail to meet the requirements of the preceding sentence solely because -

"(A) it provides for a sale in lieu of an exchange, or

"(B) the property to be acquired as replacement property was not identified under such contract before June 9, 1997."

EFFECTIVE DATE OF 1990 AMENDMENT

Section 11701(h) of Pub. L. 101-508 provided that the amendment made by that section is effective with respect to transfers after Aug. 3, 1990.

Section 11703(d)(2) of Pub. L. 101-508 provided that: "The

amendment made by paragraph (1) (amending this section) shall apply to transfers after July 18, 1984."

EFFECTIVE DATE OF 1989 AMENDMENT

Section 7601(b) of Pub. L. 101-239 provided that:

"(1) In general. - Except as provided in paragraph (2), the amendments made by this section (amending this section) shall apply to transfers after July 10, 1989, in taxable years ending after such date.

"(2) Binding contract. - The amendments made by this section shall not apply to any transfer pursuant to a written binding contract in effect on July 10, 1989, and at all times thereafter before the transfer."

EFFECTIVE DATE OF 1986 AMENDMENT

Amendment by Pub. L. 99-514 effective, except as otherwise provided, as if included in the provisions of the Tax Reform Act of 1984, Pub. L. 98-369, div. A, to which such amendment relates, see section 1881 of Pub. L. 99-514, set out as a note under section 48 of this title.

EFFECTIVE DATE OF 1984 AMENDMENT

Section 77(b) of Pub. L. 98-369, as amended by Pub. L. 99-514, Sec. 2, Oct. 22, 1986, 100 Stat. 2095, provided that:

"(1) In general. - Except as otherwise provided in this subsection, the amendment made by subsection (a) (amending this section) shall apply to transfers made after the date of the enactment of this Act (July 18, 1984) in taxable years ending after such date.

"(2) Binding contract exception for transfer of partnership interests. - Paragraph (2)(D) of section 1031(a) of the Internal Revenue Code of 1986 (formerly I.R.C. 1954) (as amended by subsection (a)) shall not apply in the case of any exchange pursuant to a binding contract in effect on March 1, 1984, and at all times thereafter before the exchange.

"(3) Requirement that property be identified within 45 days and that exchange be completed within 180 days. - Paragraph (3) of section 1031(a) of the Internal Revenue Code of 1986 (as amended by subsection (a)) shall apply -

"(A) to transfers after the date of the enactment of this Act (July 18, 1984), and

"(B) to transfers on or before such date of enactment if the property to be received in the exchange is not received before January 1, 1987.

In the case of any transfer on or before the date of the enactment of this Act which the taxpayer treated as part of a like-kind exchange, the period for assessing any deficiency of tax attributable to the amendment made by subsection (a) (amending this section) shall not expire before January 1, 1988.

"(4) Special rule where property identified in binding contract. - If the property to be received in the exchange is identified in a binding contract in effect on June 13, 1984, and at all times thereafter before the transfer, paragraph (3) shall be applied -

"(A) by substituting 'January 1, 1989' for 'January 1, 1987', and

"(B) by substituting 'January 1, 1990' for 'January 1, 1988'.

"(5) Special rule for like-kind exchange of partnership interests. - Paragraph (2)(D) of section 1031(a) of the Internal Revenue Code of 1986 (as amended by subsection (a)) shall not apply to any exchange of an interest as general partner pursuant to a plan of reorganization of ownership interest under a contract which took effect on March 29, 1984, and which was executed on or before March 31, 1984, but only if all the exchanges contemplated by the reorganization plan are completed on or before December 31, 1984."

EFFECTIVE DATE OF 1969 AMENDMENT

Section 212(c)(2) of Pub. L. 91-172, as amended by Pub. L. 99-514, Sec. 2, Oct. 22, 1986, 100 Stat. 2095, provided that: "The amendment made by paragraph (1) (amending this section) shall apply to taxable years to which the Internal Revenue Code of 1986 (formerly I.R.C. 1954) applies."

EFFECTIVE DATE OF 1959 AMENDMENT

Amendment by Pub. L. 86-346 effective for taxable years ending after Sept. 22, 1959, see section 203 of Pub. L. 86-346, set out as an Effective Date note under section 1037 of this title.

EFFECTIVE DATE OF 1958 AMENDMENT

Amendment by Pub. L. 85-866 applicable to taxable years beginning after Dec. 31, 1953, and ending after Aug. 16, 1954, see section 1(c)(1) of Pub. L. 85-866, set out as a note under section 165 of this title.

PLAN AMENDMENTS NOT REQUIRED UNTIL JANUARY 1, 1989

For provisions directing that if any amendments made by subtitle A or subtitle C of title XI (Sec. 1101-1147 and 1171-1177) or title XVIII (Sec. 1800-1899A) of Pub. L. 99-514 require an amendment to any plan, such plan amendment shall not be required to be made before the first plan year beginning on or after Jan. 1, 1989, see section 1140 of Pub. L. 99-514, as amended, set out as a note under section 401 of this title.

-SECREF-

SECTION REFERRED TO IN OTHER SECTIONS

This section is referred to in sections 83, 197, 424, 453, 454, 704, 857, 1035, 1036, 1037, 1060, 1245, 1250, 2032A, 2057 of this title.

Index

IRA WEALTH

Revolutionary IRA Strategies for Real Estate Investment
Patrick W. Rice with Jennifer Dirks

For decades, banks and brokerage houses have effectively convinced us that IRA holdings can be invested only in stocks and CDs. Then, with the sharp decline in the stock market, most of us could only stand by and watch as our retirement savings lost their accumulated value. Few knew that there was a viable alternative that offered both safety and growth. That alternative is real estate. That's right. Contrary to what you may have believed, it is perfectly legal to hold real estate investments in an IRA account—and to enjoy unprecedented returns.

For twenty years, IRA investment expert Patrick W. Rice has taught thousands of men and women his revolutionary strategies for using an IRA to create wealth based on real estate. In his new book, Mr. Rice shares these moneymaking strategies with you. He first teaches you how to turn your IRA into a self-directed account. He then details the many ways in which real estate products can make you rich, from buying rental houses, notes, and foreclosures, to building shopping centers. Mr. Rice offers a wide variety of strategies for both the aggressive investor looking for high returns, and the conservative investor interested in a steady stream of income—all tax-deferred or tax-exempt.

Although it may be a little late to avoid the volatility of the stock market, the lesson has been simple: Don't put all your eggs in one basket. Patrick Rice now offers you an entirely new basket—one that holds golden eggs for a bright and rewarding future.

$16.95 US/$27.50 CAN • 272 pages • 6 x 9-inch quality paperback • ISBN 0-7570-0094-0

RETIRING RIGHT, THIRD EDITION
Planning for a Successful Retirement
Lawrence J. Kaplan

Everybody dreams of a "golden retirement"—carefree times, financial security, and good health. But without the proper planning, that dream can turn into a nightmare. *Retiring Right* was developed to provide you with all the facts you need to design your own individual retirement plan so that you can make your special dream a reality.

Written by Dr. Lawrence J. Kaplan, one of the country's leading experts in retirement planning, this practical book answers all your most important

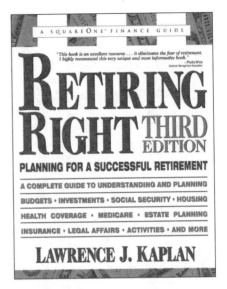

questions about savings and investment income, the Social Security system, and so much more. Each section covers a particular area of concern, including lifestyle issues such as working, leisure, and housing; long-term retirement funding, including savings and investments and pensions; day-to-day financial considerations, such as budgeting and taxes; life and health insurance; and preparing for the inevitable through estate planning, wills, and trusts. All information reflects the latest regulations so that you can take full advantage of the newest tax laws and maximize your retirement income.

Through planning guides and worksheets, *Retiring Right* helps you apply successful retirement strategies to meet your individual needs. These guides allow you to evaluate your financial situation, select and implement the means by which you can achieve financial security, and chart your course towards a fulfilling and secure retirement.

$17.95 US/$28.95 CAN • 396 pages • 7.5 x 9-inch quality paperback • 2-Color
Personal Finance/Retirement • ISBN 0-7570-0132-7